THE MOMENT

ALSO BY BAKARI SELLERS

Who Are Your People?

My Vanishing Country: A Memoir

PRAISE FOR *THE MOMENT*

"Toni Morrison once said, 'The function, the very serious function of racism is distraction.' In *The Moment*, Bakari Sellers brilliantly and precisely cuts through the noise of the calculated, well-financed, and relentless campaign by conservative media, think tanks, and politicians to end the post–George Floyd 'racial reckoning' and reverse the civil rights victories of the past fifty years. This is a must read!"

—Joy-Ann Reid, *New York Times* bestselling author
and host of MSNBC's *The ReidOut*

"Bakari Sellers takes the baton his father, Cleveland Sellers, passed to him and makes ferocious social justice strides with his new book *The Moment*. In crisp language and stellar reporting, Bakari takes us through why the recent 'racial reckoning' after the uproar of George Floyd's murder was not only the briefest in American history, but also why that brevity was not accidental. This is essential reading."

—Angela Rye

"The truth hurts. The truth also heals as evidenced in *The Moment*, Bakari Sellers's timely examination of institutional white nationalism, Black resistance and resilience, and the political and media players who are determined to keep the status quo for fear of losing their privileged roles in a rapidly changing, multi-complexioned America."

—Charlamagne tha God

"An urgent, astute synthesis of many hard truths . . . 'Spanning the Civil War and the civil rights eras,' writes Sellers, 'this country has experienced two reconstructions followed by a white supremacist pushback against each,' and the author links this to post-Obama voter suppression. 'The supporters of white supremacist philosophy—whether they be Donald Trump, Jesse Watters, Megyn Kelly, Mitch McConnell, or others—want to maintain all the power.' In impressively concise fashion, Sellers makes a host of pertinent arguments crisply and effectively, disturbingly documenting the overtness of efforts to maintain structural racism across the country."

—*Kirkus Reviews* (starred review)

"Brother Bakari Sellers is determined to look past the many distractions of our public discourse to see the potential for an America that works for all of us. In this book he not only shines a light on the lies that are being used to divide Americans; he offers real hope that this moment might be the beginning of a Third Reconstruction."

—Rev. Dr. William J. Barber II, author of *White Poverty: How Exposing Myths About Race and Class Can Reconstruct American Democracy*

"In *The Moment*, Bakari Sellers manages to capture the frustration and struggles felt by those who are dedicated to fighting inequality while offering hope for the future. The book is essential for anyone seeking to understand the evolution of the civil rights movement as well as the political, social, and economic obstacles that prevent racial progress."

—Michael Harriot, author of *Black AF History: The Un-Whitewashed Story of America*

THOUGHTS ON THE RACE

RECKONING THAT WASN'T

THE MOMENT

AND HOW WE ALL CAN

MOVE FORWARD NOW

———

BAKARI
SELLERS

AMISTAD

An Imprint of HarperCollinsPublishers

HarperCollins books may be purchased for educational, business, or sales promotional use. For information, please email the Special Markets Department at SPsales@harpercollins.com.

FIRST HARPERCOLLINS PAPERBACK EDITION PUBLISHED IN 2025

Designed by Leah Carlson-Stanisic

Library of Congress Cataloging-in-Publication Data is available upon request.

ISBN 978-0-06-308503-9

25 26 27 28 29 LBC 5 4 3 2 1

To my children, nieces, and nephews—and all the founders of SNCC. This book is about standing on the shoulders of giants and boldly looking toward the future.

CONTENTS

BEHIND THE PHOTOGRAPH

Oftentimes, I find myself staring down at an image of seven young Black men wearing trench coats; the black-and-white photograph is particularly special to me, considering the recent passing of one of the men in the photo, the legendary actor Harry Belafonte. Also included in the picture are future congressman John Lewis; Bill Hall; my father, Cleve Sellers; Willie Ricks; James Forman; and Sidney Poitier. Apart from the two entertainment celebrities, all the men were part of the Student Nonviolent Coordinating Committee (SNCC) during the civil rights era. The picture was taken just after Harry Belafonte and Sidney Poitier posted $250 bond for the men to be released from jail.

Earlier that day, on March 21, 1966, decades before the launch of an international anti-apartheid movement, Daddy, John Lewis, and the other SNCC men had walked into the South African consulate's office in New York to protest the barbaric racial segregation system in that country. Days prior to their arrest, they had marched into the

South African embassy in Washington, DC, demanding to speak to the ambassador to protest South African atrocities, including the violent attack on demonstrators in 1960 known as the Sharpeville massacre, during which 249 protesters—50 of which were women and children—were shot, wounded, or killed by white South African police.

Back in New York City, Daddy recalled, the men "demanded to speak to the South African consulate general, but the police were called and arrested all of us." As the police began to transport them to Rikers Island, John Lewis called Belafonte, a New York native, and that's when Belafonte and Sidney Poitier rushed over to bail them out. Lewis and Forman, both top SNCC officials, would often call on a prominent Black man like Belafonte to help. Why? Because there was nobody else to call. African Americans were mostly in this battle alone, and my father believes we're still in it alone.

I once asked him how he feels about our present times, when so much of what he fought for in the 1960s is being ripped away. "We are back to the starting point," Dad said. "We are at about 1954. We thought everything was becoming so good for us, that we were flying along thinking we were doing all kinds of good things, romanticizing our plight. But there's nothing romantic about our plight, about our situation, and we must get back to the drawing board because nobody is going to fight and win victories for the African American community but the African American community."

And that's the reason this picture sticks out to me. And it is also why I wrote this book. The photo is the embodiment of the movement, the embodiment of SNCC, the embodiment of

Black people fighting for change and against injustices. It's also a cross section of Black people coming together, similar to what we saw during the Obama campaign, of entertainment people meeting popular culture—the proverbial rubber meeting the road. During the civil rights period, as in this photograph, you'd often see esteemed entertainers with average folk like my dad, all joined together for a common cause: to raise awareness and to fight for what they believed was right.

My father often observes that with one fell swoop, Black celebrities today with great wealth, like Kanye West, could have helped fix so many Black issues, but they squandered the opportunity. However, I say there are a lot of individuals who are meeting this moment, and most of what they do you've never even heard about. You don't know the work that Will Smith is doing because he doesn't talk about it, or what Charles Barkley does, or Shaquille O'Neal or Beyoncé and Jay-Z. There are a lot of celebrities putting their shoulders into this moment, but I am one who doesn't believe people with money are obligated to help. The way I look at it, if you want to be rich and have a Ferrari, a Porsche, and a Tesla and live in a gated community and not contribute, that's fine with me—literally, it is. Because if you don't want to be a part of the movement, if you don't feel like that's your place, I'm not going to knock you. Believe me, I know there are a lot of individuals who are narrow-minded about the "fact" that they pulled themselves up by the so-called bootstraps, which is just a bullshit concept. The same people believe they got theirs, and now you must get your own.

I am going to respect their decisions. Why? Because we must

love our neighbors even when they don't love us—yes, even in our highly commodified era. We must cultivate an unabridged type of love. We must resist feeling resentful, despite all the stress and pressure to do just that. I admit I don't have the same set of expectations my father has, but I have hope. If you want to be part of the movement, then welcome. If you don't, then we will just step around or march right over you.

*　*　*

The cherished photograph reminds me that there are always pockets of hope: millennial brothers like me joining hands with celebrities who have new venture capital funds or have established new entities to help squash injustice. There is a reemergence of Black people coming together. The burden of change today is happening for a reason. In this very moment, in ways we haven't seen in more than a generation, Black people's humanity is being attacked. We can't allow that to happen. As Dr. Martin Luther King once said, "Injustice anywhere is a threat to justice everywhere."

*　*　*

There's no greater example of our African culture, specifically our southern Black heritage, than South Carolina's Gullah Geechee community. These Black Americans, descendants of West Africans enslaved on the Sea Island plantations, maintained their African heritage, their religion, and some of their ancestral language. Since slavery, they've maintained not only their cuisine but also their broad ways of life. Even with the advent of technology, even as people tried to rip away their culture, they've resisted. The problem they're having now, though, is that they still own something very valuable in this country. And you see the forces trying to take that away from them. That thing is land—valuable land that's been theirs for as long as we've been free in this country.

There's a direct line between Josephine Wright, a ninety-four-year-old great-grandmother who lived in the Lowcountry of South Carolina until her death earlier this year, and the Africans who were brought to this same land in chains to live a life of servitude. And that's why her story shows us how far we have yet to go.

The land Josephine Wright lived on had been in her family since the end of slavery, but 150 years later developers tried to take the land away by filing lawsuits against her and constructing unwelcome intrusions, including a road only feet from her modest home.

The case of Josephine Wright, who was barely five feet tall, is emblematic of the plight of Black folk today. There's always some group, some entity, trying to take what is most valuable to us, ultimately threatening our collective strength to hold on to our freedoms, rights, and humanity.

Josephine's land was passed down to her late husband, who was Gullah Geechee but lived in New York City until he retired as a lawyer thirty years ago and built the modest home in which she lived until her death. The home became a place for their extended family to gather, to celebrate birthdays, and even to say goodbye to a loved one. It's the place in which her forty grandchildren, fifty-four great-grandchildren, and sixteen great-great-grandchildren come together, but now a company has come to try to take the land—even though it's not theirs to take. And instead of treating Josephine with dignity, the company tried to bully and dehumanize her—like many of these outfits that come in to steal ancestral land from Black people in the South. The company bought up 1.8 acres all around Josephine's home and has started to develop a large subdivision. Meanwhile, she had publicly said unwelcome and unexplained things started happening: trees were cut down on her property, and a snake was found hanging over her window.

To understand that what happened to Josephine is not unusual, we must go back in time. After the Civil War ended, some slave owners in South Carolina gave their former slaves land, while other Black people worked hard to purchase their lands, which they have since passed down from one generation to the next. The beautiful marsh-filled waterside properties represent a powerful source of pride for residents because these are the most valuable assets they will ever own. Meanwhile, as Hilton Head Island transformed into a hot vacation spot, unsavory developers began to take advantage of legal loopholes to steal millions of acres of land that Black families have owned for 150 years.

As developers discovered, Josephine was the last person you should mess with. When the company filed a lawsuit against her, claiming the land, Josephine collected herself and went straight to the local media. I read about her story one day on X, formerly known as Twitter (a platform that's turned to trash since Elon Musk bought it). When I read Josephine's story, I was reminded of my own grandmother. I put out a simple tweet that said "If anybody has any contact information, please give it to me." A reporter from *The Post and*

Courier, out of Charleston, sent me a note connecting me with Josephine and her grandchildren.

*   *   *

Hilton Head has what I call two-or-three-shirt weather. The humidity and heat are so strong you're bound to change shirts a few times a day because you'll sweat right through whatever you're wearing. After my first meeting with Josephine, I told her we would organize a press conference to raise awareness. I didn't need to be Josephine's lawyer, she had already found a capable lawyer, but as an influencer I could spread the word about what was happening to her and shine a light on something that had been going on in the Lowcountry for a very long time.

The Associated Press news service came to our press conference and picked up the story. We had drummers, we had experts on estate law and inheritances, but even more importantly, we had Josephine.

*   *   *

There are images of us in newspapers that make me laugh to this day. Because my six-foot-five build is too large to fit in a frame with her, my head is cut off in each photograph. But I'm not claiming this is a David and Goliath story, because this isn't really a mismatch.

Josephine might have been ninety-four, and she might have been small, but she was strong as hell. She didn't need assistance. She drove. Her thoughts were her own. "God got her," as we say. She was very faith-driven, like many individuals in the Lowcountry. And that shouldn't be surprising when you think about it because when you're stripped of everything you have, when you're deprived of your culture, your dignity, and your humanity, many times the only thing you have left, particularly for Black folk, is faith.

And so, whenever we get punched in the mouth, we as a people never give in because we've always had that faith that we'll get through. And Josephine is a perfect example of that. She spoke with great clarity when she said she wants her great-grandbaby to live on the land one day with her future children and her children's future children.

Josephine reminds me of my grandmother. When I'm around her, I don't even think of cursing; I just find myself saying, "Yes, ma'am" and "No, ma'am." I open doors for her, I want to fight for her, I want to live for her, and I just want to do right by her.

Not only did we get Josephine's GoFundMe started, which provided her with tens of thousands of dollars for legal help, but I was also able to connect her to Tyler Perry, Kyrie Irving, and Snoop Dogg, who all came to her aid. In other words, a community of Black folk empathized with her struggle, and we all came together for her. And this is the only way that we can overcome. It's the only way that any of our brothers or sisters who are going through this level of segregation and degradation can overcome this: by fighting together.

If Josephine stood for anything, it's perseverance, which is exactly what we must do in this moment of time as well. We must fight by utilizing the mediums available. Although X has few redeeming qualities these days, I still noticed a glimmer of what it used to be, small bastions of hope. After all, I was able to connect with Josephine through that medium.

We've got to examine the tools that we have, we must be extremely vigilant, and we must be selfless to some extent—we have to be willing to give more of ourselves. And we must take these moments where we can put our shoulder to the wheel for our loved ones and help. If Josephine Wright's family can keep her land, it's going to mean something very important to entire generations of her family. Years from now, they can take a loan out against it, but even more importantly, it's going to give them a sense of self that they own something. You know, many people don't own anything; they may own their car but nothing of significance. But if Josephine Wright's family can hold on to a little piece of something, that's going to build confidence, and it will give them a leg up on something that many Black people still don't have: a fair chance to build wealth.

* * *

My father, who nearly died in a racial massacre in 1968 and was in the middle of so much of our history, was an organizer during the dangerous Freedom Summer in Mississippi. I'm concerned that he believes we are truly going backward. He points to the targeted killings of Black people in Jacksonville, Buffalo, and Charleston and says we're seeing a new system of violence in America. "We've just been through that period in which the police were the ones killing us, and now it's turned to something else." Groups like the Proud Boys, he says, are multiplying and entrenched, and that's where we are going to start seeing more violence.

Dad is soft-spoken and kind, but he doesn't mince words regarding how bad things are, how backward things have gotten. "We have to persevere," he says.

And he's right. The opportunities that we won through the

hard work my father and so many Black people did during the civil rights era are no longer available to the African American community. My father's generation accomplished the Voting Rights Act of 1965 and the Fair Housing Act of 1968, and they achieved all of this with their blood in the streets, but now we see an erosion of those policies and of our civil liberties. Now we see the Supreme Court striking down affirmative action, and states banning Black history books and persecuting Black scholars and authors. We live in a world now where a writer like the great James Baldwin would have to fight to exist. Can you imagine Baldwin debating Ron DeSantis?

So, like the old folk used to say a long time ago, "We need to put on our boots and blue jeans" and get back to developing a social and moral consciousness within the African American community.

We are the ones who will determine our destiny. We must go back and begin to talk about organizing like those seven men in the photograph had done throughout the civil rights era. And there's one thing I'm damn sure about: the unique element and the tie that binds us all is our resilience, which is found in our faith, our togetherness, and our shared history of struggle, like Josephine and the Gullah people in the Lowcountry.

* * *

When I look at that black-and-white photograph, I see seven Black men of strong bearing, standing toes down (as we say in the South) for what they believe in. Everyone in the photograph is looking in different directions. John Lewis is looking down, while, of course, Sidney Poitier is staring directly into the camera. My father is looking into an abyss, probably wondering how mad his parents were going to be. But those young Black men back then—maybe it wasn't every single Black man on every single corner, but it was a few of them— joined together arm in arm for a common good, for a higher purpose, to fight injustice.

*   *   *

We're living during a moment in time when the system still does not allow the right to vote. Someone will always say, "Wait, we can still vote. We just don't have the same freedom to vote as when the Voting Rights Act was passed."

But my response is that voting is a right. That's what people miss. It is a right, and no one should be able to take it away by making it difficult to vote because of your location, because of some document, or because there's a pandemic. It is your fundamental right just for merely existing.

So, what I am saying is that this country does not allow the democracy that was promised. America is not living up to its constitutional vision. I wrote this book because we have to find ways in which we can empower the African American community so that we can be a part of creating a democracy in its truest form and creating a world where my children not only can live in a better America for African Americans and other disfranchised people but also will be equipped to help develop a world where human existence is equitable—forever.

1

THE MOMENT

The morning I broke down emotionally on national television, I recalled a quote from Ella Baker, the behind-the-scenes mastermind of the civil rights movement. Over five decades, she worked with W. E. B. Du Bois, Thurgood Marshall, and Martin Luther King and counseled young activists like Bob Moses, Diane Nash, Stokely Carmichael, and my father, Cleveland Sellers.

Ella died in 1986 when I was only two, but I lived at my father's knee as a child, meaning I inhaled all of the wisdom, trials, and triumphs of the Student Nonviolent Coordinating Committee, which my father had been a part of since the 1960s. Miss Baker was truly a "shero" of my dad's. She poured a great amount into young men like him who would become heroes and legends themselves.

I tried to remember some of her famous words, believing they would be appropriate to recite on television for a live segment I was about to do for CNN. I'm certain that Miss Baker's heart would have ached not only for George Floyd but for all the events that were happening at that moment in spring 2020. The nation was on fire, and we were isolated in a global pandemic. There was trouble in the land: protests and unrest were erupting all over the country and all around the world.

We couldn't avoid the truth: America had to change.

* * *

By the time George Floyd was murdered by a Minneapolis police officer on May 25, 2020, we were almost sixty days into the pandemic. Our routines were disrupted. The country had stopped, everybody was watching the news, but the news had changed because the people reporting and commenting on the news were now doing so from their kitchens or basements; journalists and anchors had studio setups in their homes. Very few people were in the studios at CNN. I was doing a lot of television at the time because of the election—I'm a political analyst for CNN—but I was also on a virtual tour for my first book.

My makeshift studio was set up in our home, which was tough because I had toddlers running around the house. Like most Black folk, our dining room was used only on Easter and Thanksgiving, but it had a big round table and a side table, which were perfect for me to set up "my studio." I'd sit in front of my computer with a dress shirt, tie, jacket, and pajama pants.

Three days after Floyd's death, I headed to my makeshift studio for a CNN broadcast. I was up that morning around 6 a.m. to get ready. It was not an unusual routine: When our twins, Stokely and Sadie, wake up, we put them in our bed. That morning, they stayed in the bed with my wife, Ellen. Kai, our oldest daughter, was in virtual school and would be up by 8:15. The childcare worker was usually at the house by 8.

As I stepped over the baby gate and into my makeshift studio, I turned on my studio light and connected to CNN with my laptop. CNN never tells you what questions they'll ask; they just tell you the topic, and I knew I was going to be talking about George Floyd. For me, Floyd's killing was a buildup because we had recently seen the video of Ahmaud Arbery. We had already known the name of Breonna Taylor, and we knew that a lot of poor people, and particularly Black folk, were suffering and dying in disproportionate numbers during the pandemic.

I'll say it simply: I believed George Floyd's death, for a lot of us, was the proverbial straw that broke the camel's back.

As I was sitting down waiting, Ella Baker's quote came to me, but I couldn't remember all of it. I knew I wanted to talk about 1964. One of the issues I wanted people to understand is that George Floyd's death may be un-American; it may be unbelievable, heartbreaking, tragic—it may be every adjective that you can think of—but it's not new. I always try to draw on some historical reference, and for this conversation, the historical figure I knew would provide wisdom was Ella Baker.

What was it that Ella Baker said?

Like so many who had the privilege of knowing her, my father remembered Ella Baker as a brilliant sage who always dressed proper and was kind and extremely eloquent. She was also a shrewd and strategic grassroots organizer who advised my father and the other activists like "Uncle" Stokely Carmichael, who traveled to Mississippi to register Black people to vote, on how not to get killed. She warned them to avoid in-terracial dating and to keep their middle-class ways to them-selves. They needed to look and act like the locals. "You should have seen Stokely pushing a plow," my father often said with a laugh.

*　　*　　*

What was it that Ella said?

Because I was logged on to CNN, I could hear and watch the segment on the air before me: George Floyd's brother Philonise was talking to Alisyn Camerota, then coanchor of CNN's flagship morning show, *New Day*.

"Joining us now is Philonise Floyd, the brother of George Floyd, and their family's attorney, Benjamin Crump," Camer-ota said. "Philonise, thank you very much for taking the time to be with us this morning. We're really sorry for your family's loss. We know that you are all deeply grieving right now. But when you see what has happened overnight in Minneapolis because of the anger and outrage about your brother's death, what are your thoughts this morning?"

Wearing a purple button-down shirt, Philonise Floyd looked like George Floyd, his older brother. He was espe-cially polite to the anchor and spoke passionately and from the heart about his brother's recent death. "Well, I want ev-erybody to understand that it's just like a child searching for attention. [The protesters] have been doing everything posi-tive, and nobody is listening. And all of a sudden, they start acting out. So, I want everybody to be peaceful right now, but people are torn and hurt because they're tired of seeing Black men die constantly over and over again," he said. "You know, I spoke to Eric Garner's mom and Rev. Al Sharpton, and her son couldn't breathe. He kept saying he couldn't breathe. And my brother said the same thing, that he couldn't breathe. And nobody cared. And these officers, they need to be arrested right now. They need to be arrested and held accountable about everything. Because these people [the protesters] want justice right now."

The anchor asked, "And what is justice for your family? What does that look like?"

At that very moment, Philonise Floyd lowered his head and shook it. "Justice is these guys need to be arrested, convicted of murder, and given the death penalty. They need to, because they took my brother's life. He will never get that back. I will never see him again. My family will never see him again. His kids will never see him again."

"Have you watched that video of your brother's arrest?" Camerota asked.

"I watched the video. It was hard," Floyd replied. "But I had to watch the video. And as I watched the video, those four officers, they executed my brother. The paramedics, they drug my brother across the ground without administering CPR. They showed no empathy, no compassion. Nobody out there showed it. Nobody."

He told her that every time he looks up, he sees on television the video of his brother dying as a police officer kneels on his neck. As Ben Crump, Floyd's attorney, started to describe his brother's gruesome death, Floyd lowered his head again, rubbed his tearful eyes, and sobbed.

As I watched Floyd break down, I was like, *Man, I'm not going to be able to make it.* I knew how emotional I was.

I told myself, *Bakari, just remain steadfast, remain true, and you'll be okay.*

I don't like crying because people tell me I cry too much. I also hate it because my voice gets so high-pitched and I can never bring it down, no matter how much I try, and the pitch drives me insane. But I don't stop the crying because I don't care what people think. I'd cried once before on CNN, back when I was with Don Lemon and they kind of surprised me when they played the clip of the Reverend Clementa Pinckney's funeral. Clementa, a friend, was one of the nine people killed by a self-described white supremacist in 2015 at the Mother Emanuel AME Church in Charleston, South Carolina.

*   *   *

What did Ella say?

At last, as I was about to go on air, I remembered the Ella Baker quote.

CNN anchor John Berman introduced me and former NFL wide receiver and commentator Donté Stallworth. "Gentlemen," he said, "it's not easy to watch Philonise Floyd talk about his brother, but think about how hard it is to watch the video of his brother dying while pleading for his life. And Bakari, a couple words that Philonise used again and again: 'tired.' He's tired of this and then nobody is listening."

I went over Ella Baker's quote in my head. She talked about the value of a Black life, which is what I wanted to start off with. "Yes," I replied. "Ella Baker said, 'Until the killing of Black men, Black mothers' sons, becomes as important to the rest of the country as the killing of a white mother's son, we who believe in freedom cannot rest until this happens.'"

After I repeated her quote, I realized her words summarized the way that I felt. I was weary, I was tired. I knew I could not rest.

"She said that in 1964. And we're still echoing those same cries today," I said. "It was hard to listen to that interview."

At my mention of Philonise Floyd, I touched my ear and bit my lip. I can always feel when I am about to weep because I will have this long swallow and I can feel my face swelling up. What I've learned over time is that I must talk through it. I just go ahead and don't pause because the tears will go nowhere, they will still flow, so I just talk through it and try to breathe.

"It's just so much pain. You get so tired. We have Black children. I have a fifteen-year-old daughter. I mean, what do I tell her? I'm raising a son. I have no idea what to tell him. It's just—it's hard being Black in this country when your life is not valued, and people are worried about the protesters and the looters."

I saw my son, Stokely, on the ground. I could only imagine what George had to be going through for him to call out for his mother. After I had recited Ella's quote, I thought about my daughter Kai, because her birthday was June 1, and she was going to turn fifteen; she would be learning to drive, and that was the biggest conversation going in our household. How do we prepare her to drive and talk to her about the police? For me, it was difficult to think about this and watch this George Floyd incident. What do we tell Black children? I thought about my father, who was shot by South Carolina state troopers in 1968, and I thought about the three young Black men who were killed that night.

"And it's just people who are frustrated, who, for far too long, have not had their voices heard," I continued. "And so, you put me on after his brother. And I feel like I lost *my* brother."

·   ·   ·

As a child, I sat in churches and at events, watching my father discuss all the people he saw die during the civil rights years. So much death, so much hate and violence. He always let his tears flow, and there I was, a little boy listening to every word and crying with him.

"And nobody cares about the video," I told the CNN audience. "They had a video with Ahmaud Arbery, and two different solicitors looked at that video and declined to press charges. And so, for those of us who have a mistrust of the system, it's very hard for us to do anything else other than just to cry this morning and then hope and pray that we're not sitting next to Ben Crump one day. That's about all we can do."

Berman then asked, "Bakari, your father was shot more than fifty years ago. Fifty years ago. And we're sitting here this morning and watching it happen again. So where do you find the hope? How do you tell your son and daughters that it's going to get better?"

I stared off into the distance as I mindlessly played with my quarantine beard. My eyes were red. "I don't know," I responded. "I tried to keep hope. I try to keep faith. I keep telling my children they can be free. You know, I want my kids to one day be able to grow up and be the host of *New Day*. I want them to be able to be a United States senator or a president. But what happens if they get pulled over and they comply? What happens if they get judged by a father and a son who just are on a good old-fashioned Georgia lynching? What happens if they get served a no-knock warrant, like Breonna Taylor? I mean, what happens if that—how do you raise your children in this America to understand you're free when we see these images of them being gunned down in the street and the knee in the back of the neck for eight minutes like a dog?" I shrugged and rubbed my beard. "So, I don't have that answer other than every day, I just tell them I love them. That's all I can do."

I looked to the left of my computer screen, toward my bedroom where my twins were asleep. Upstairs, Kai was either sleeping or preparing for school. After the interview concluded, I lay down in the bed with my kids and Ellen, as we always do, and the morning proceeded. I did not know how many people saw the CNN interview or that it was a viral moment until a few people called or texted me from CNN. They wanted to tell me how happy they were that I was at the network or how thankful they were to have me, and then I saw the interview everywhere.

The moment not only went viral (nearly a million views on YouTube, 744,000 hits on Twitter, 2 million hits on Facebook), but it became a global touch and data point. It was clear that my thoughts had struck a chord, but the moment on CNN had a mixed reaction in the Black community. The overwhelming majority of people were proud that I could be vulnerable and lead with my voice. But some had the opposite reaction. As I was finishing the book tour, one guy phoned in to a radio show and called me everything but a child of God. "Don't get up there and be crying on TV," he told me. "I don't know why we let you coons get up there and cry. We got to be strong. We got to fight back."

But what I think we must understand is just because you share emotion doesn't mean you're docile. You can be righteously angry and fight back. I was angry, very angry.

On Twitter, a lot of people were commenting. The most common sentiment was "I wish I could hug Bakari right now." Those hugs are good, but you don't have to hug me. I wish that, as a country, we could wrap our arms around the young Black boys and girls who have to live with this trauma. It goes back to the fact that when you're Black and have a platform, it's unjust not to use your platform to speak your truth to power. Now I know everybody doesn't do it and that's their own thing, but I just think that we don't have that privilege. For athletes or entertainers or commentators or pastors or whatever, we just don't have that privilege to sit on our hands and say that we're not going to talk about this or that. We must talk about the issues that affect us because if we don't, then a lot of people will take that as acquiescence. For many, that acquiescence or that silence is a free pass to keep killing us.

To the extent my tears were a metaphoric and collective scream in the form of a viral moment, so be it. America needed change, and if I know anything for sure, it's that the only way to cope with change is to create it.

2

DEAR STOKELY

As I start to write these words to you, my son, please know that you are my little "Man Man." Only two and some change, you have just walked down the steps outside the house by yourself. You're looking fresh in your Spider-Man shirt (that's the only kind of shirt you will wear these days), red shorts, red Adidas sneakers, and white socks pulled up high like you're somebody's uncle. If this was another day, you might have stumbled or held my hand or turned and crawled backward down the stairs, but not this time. For some reason, today you put one foot in front of the other and did it. I said, "Good job, buddy," like I was talking to my boys, Pop, or Jarrod, and then you did a little jig.

My sweet Stokely, I'm sitting down writing these words to you while you are still a toddler. But I'm writing for a much older you, for a time in the future as you move from boy to man, a time when I can tell you about the man you are named after, Stokely Carmichael, one of my many "uncles."

Stokely, you are a precious child and my only son. I am writing this chapter to you because I believe it's always important that we pour more into our Black boys. We should do it consciously and intentionally. I must be willful in my efforts to ensure that you know that you're loved. The plight of the Black man in today's "New" South, in today's America, in today's world, requires us to do just this and more than ever. And so, my words to you are meant to ensure that you understand the love, the guidance, and the support that are necessary for you to go out and become the leader of whichever household you choose and also to become the leader of a community and to become the impactful and positive change your father wishes to see in this moment but may not.

· · ·

Your namesake, Stokely Carmichael, and your granddaddy Cleveland Sellers were major civil rights leaders during the 1960s and beyond. Stokely was your granddaddy's best friend; they were roommates at Howard University before they became revolutionaries, before they began to fight for the rights of our people.

When your granddad was only nineteen, he traveled along with Uncle Stokely and many other young people to Mississippi to search for three young activists and Freedom workers who had disappeared. Granddad said some people believed the young men were just missing, but he knew better because hate and viciousness were everywhere in Mississippi.

Even if you never learn about them in school, I need you to remember the names of the three activists: James Chaney, Andrew Goodman, and Michael "Mickey" Schwerner.

During that "long, hot summer," my dad knew death could come from a firebomb, a police officer whipping, or a lynch-

ing. Only "dumb luck," Dad said, kept him and the other young volunteers alive. He recalls the pain in his stomach when the FBI found the bodies of James, Andrew, and Mickey. "PTSD is real," he recently told me. The excruciating pain caused by their deaths "plagued" his mind and stayed with him for several days, but I wonder if that anxiety has ever gone away.

Stokely, faith and fear cannot coexist. But this feeling will not arrive without emotional risks.

With all the deaths I've known of young Black men, I've inherited Daddy's anxiety, maybe because our family has always carried the community on its shoulders. It goes back to my two grandfathers; they were giants—strong believers in family and in men, particularly Black men, being our bedrock.

I think a lot of my grandfathers' strength came from the fact that they weren't ever scared to allow the women in their worlds to shine, to achieve their highest levels of whatever it may be. My grandmothers were both amazing women, centerpieces of their communities, and their husbands stood behind them and supported them. But I say all that to explain that it started with my grandfathers; they both believed this country is worth fighting for, that it's not irredeemable, but it's so imperfect.

My mama's father was E. W. Williamson, who we kids called Pawpa. He was a tall, chocolate man, who wore his naturally wavy hair slicked back. He was nearly six-foot-three, wore only suits, and always drove a Cadillac. He was also one of the most prominent Black ministers in Memphis, always preaching from the Baptist pulpit, attempting to get people to their necessary spiritual strength so they could effectuate change in their communities.

He was also part of a political group of four Black preachers *in Memphis called the Four Horsemen. These men did all they could to assist the young civil rights activists in the 1960s. One of the horsemen was Benjamin Hooks. "Uncle Benjamin" and his wife, "Aunt Frances," as Mama called them, were your grand-mama's godparents.*

Stokely, I am not sure your classmates will get to read about Benjamin Hooks in school, but I want you to know he was a great man; he later became the legendary NAACP director. He was also your great-grandfather's friend from way back.

In fact, Uncle Benjamin often preached at Greater Middle Baptist Church under Pawpa, so when Pawpa was about to leave Memphis to go pastor at an even larger church in Chi-cago, he asked the congregation in Memphis to accept Benja-min Hooks as their full-time pastor. You hear about these Black churches splitting up behind a preacher leaving, but Pawpa said, "I'd really appreciate it if we could do this unanimously." And they did.

Mama remembers civil rights leaders like Ralph Abernathy and Martin Luther King eating dinner at the house in Memphis and staying for several days while they were in town. According to Mama, my grandma would clap her hands and say, "We are going to set a fine table tonight 'cause so-and-so is coming over." The Irish linen, Waterford crystal, china dinner plates, and silverware came out of the linen closet and onto the table.

"They were all SCLC [Southern Christian Leadership Confer-ence] people," Mama recalls. "My daddy didn't have great love for SNCC at all. Coretta [Scott King] came a couple of times. She and Mother enjoyed each other's company. They would disap-pear and go talk girly talk or whatever. Rev. Samuel Billy Kyles would come over too, though he lived in Memphis. In the picture

where King was standing on the balcony of the Lorraine Motel before he was assassinated, the person standing next to him, on one side of him, is Billy Kyles."

*   *   *

My grandparents lived in a cul-de-sac called Melrose Cove, which was made up of eleven ranch-style homes. Mama said Pawpa and ten other Black families bought the land together. "They were all of like mind, and so they did not mind living amongst each other," she said. "When one added this huge family room across the back—I think that was Dr. Watson on the corner—next thing you know, everybody in the Cove was adding these huge family rooms in the back."

Because I am younger than my siblings, I depend on your uncle and aunt for details of our visits with Grandma and Pawpa in Memphis. As children, we'd stay in Memphis for a month. We slept in the living room, but your uncle Lumumba swears our Pawpa did not sleep. Lumumba would wake up and see Pawpa walking around the house, talking to himself, praying all the time. He would be clapping, praying, singing. He would also wake up early and record his radio messages on the tape recorder. He'd preach on this little tape recorder like it was a regular Sunday service. When we were young, Lumumba remembers, we were like, "Oh my God, when are you going to sleep?"

But many years later, we realized Pawpa was living a life of prayer. He not only preached it, but he lived it.

Mama explained what was going on with Pawpa. "It may have seemed like to you children that he never slept because you were little, but Daddy slept," she said. "He would take naps in the middle of the day if he could. I knew that because Ms. Minnie T. Payne, who helped Mama with the house, would always fuss about it. She'd tell my mother, 'I just cannot get Reverend to stay off of that bed after I made it up.' I recall Mama saying, 'Just make it up once.'"

Your grandmother agrees Pawpa would walk through the house and sing because he used the time for meditation and reflection. "Our house was so lively most of the time," she told me, "so he had to wait until other folks went to sleep to have his time."

When we rolled into Memphis from out of town, we'd put our bags down and everybody would gather in the living room, make a circle, and hold hands. He would thank God for us arriving safely. When we were about to travel back to South Carolina, we'd go into the living room and hold hands, and he'd pray for the next time they'd see us again.

If anybody had a problem in the Black community, whether it was a problem with a child, with their finances, or with their car, they called Pawpa first.

And my paternal grandfather, Granddaddy Sellers, was very similar, though on the surface he couldn't be more different than Pawpa. Daddy's father didn't wear suits and wasn't no minister, but he was a country businessman who owned property, mostly small houses throughout Denmark, South Carolina, along with the only taxi service and Denmark's only motel, which we still own.

When people needed money or had problems, they came to Granddaddy Sellers. He believed that our path to equality had everything to do with having economic sustainability in our communities. A dark-skinned man with sun-worn skin and

rough hands and gnarled fingers, Granddaddy hustled, work-
ing as a part-time farmer, taxi driver, and restaurant owner.
Eventually, he'd build and own dozens of houses throughout
Denmark.

Daddy recalls when he was a little boy, Granddaddy Sellers
worked all the time, but he also tried to come home early just to
play with him. Your paternal granddaddy grew up in poverty,
which is probably why he made sure Daddy and Aunt Gwendo-
lyn didn't want for anything. Daddy was raised in the segregated
South, where every business was Black-owned, the schools were
Black, the churches he attended were Black, and all Granddad-
dy's customers were Black.

*   *   *

Stokely, Dad started preparing me to become what he called "a
change agent" when I was younger than you are now.

I was still in your grandmother's belly when he leaned close to
Mama to tell me about the time he was shot by patrol officers on
February 8, 1968, during the Orangeburg massacre. Throughout
my childhood, Daddy made me his shadow. He took me to all
his speaking engagements, all the rallies, and all the Orange-
burg massacre memorials.

I realize now that he gave me a blueprint that I plan to fol-
low to raise you to also be an activist. Every chance he got, he
taught me about the struggles our people faced throughout his-
tory and are still forced to endure today. But he also let me know
we do not have to be victims of oppression by showing me what
greatness and fighting for justice look like. He introduced me to
my brilliant "uncles" and "aunties" named Stokely Carmichael,
Jesse Jackson, Julian Bond, and Kathleen Cleaver. My father

gave me the tools and the freedom to figure out my place in the world, accepting whatever I chose to do in life but expecting I'd use my skills to uplift my community.

By the time you are old enough to understand this letter, you too will know what greatness looks like: you will have seen the photograph of your dad and President Barack Obama, and the photograph of your grandfather, Martin Luther King, and your Uncle Stokely sitting with President Lyndon Johnson as he signed the Civil Rights Act of 1964.

You'll know I was the youngest Black elected official not only in the South Carolina House of Representatives but in the country. I will share my journey for justice with you, taking you to my speaking engagements and to the set of CNN. Just like my dad did for me, I will make you my shadow. I will do this not to add pressure, but so you can experience the possibilities of what you too can be. That is all I want for you and your sisters, Sadie and Kai: to develop an activist mindset and to see brave and determined men and women in action. For me, I had to see Black lawyers and Black politicians before I knew I could be one.

My only demand is that whatever you decide to be, use your skills to help change the world. I want you to have the freedom to dictate how you will change the world, whether it will be as a lawyer like your father, a doctor like your aunt Nosizwe, or a minister and business executive like your uncle Cleveland Lumumba, or whatever you want to be. But you must work to make a change, as the enduring inequalities demand it.

While we have made progress through the years, we have yet to reach the mountaintop. In America, the criminal and environmental justice systems are broken. The education and prison systems are also in shambles. As I write this, I just learned about *a case where the Ohio court system sentenced a Black woman to prison for eighteen months but a white woman, convicted of the same exact charges, got probation, even though she had a record of committing more crimes than the Black woman.*

All of this is occurring as we are still in the middle of a global pandemic, which has disproportionately impacted African Americans. Meanwhile, Republicans are aggressively trying to take away the voting rights of mostly Black and Brown people. So, you see, there is much work to do. Unfortunately, I'm sure there will be as much work to do when you are old enough to read this letter. Still, I hope by then that I have raised you to be unapologetically and proudly Black. If there is a segment of white America that won't see you as a human entitled to equal rights, opportunities, and respect, do know they are wrong. They fear your greatness, our people's greatness.

This means we must work to rebuild America into a place that will give you the benefit of your humanity. How do we do that? We must set the stage for a new generation to continue the struggle, and I am starting with you, Stokely. That's what we must do, and it must start with planting seeds earlier than we ever thought in our own Black sons.

As you continue your education to strengthen your knowledge and have experiences to hone your skills, it's my task to continue my work to ensure we will be living in a country where you will be free to use what you learned to make a better world. It is important to understand this urgency I live with now, and you will need to address it when it is your time. It has little to do with anyone saying the word "nigger" more than they did a few years ago, but it has everything to do with the systemic levels of oppression that our people are still dealing with.

* * *

Stokely, the health-care system continues to be broken. Five hours after you and your sister were born, I sat with the two of you as your mother fought for her life. It is tragic, at this current time, my dear son, that Black women are still dying at alarming rates due to complications of childbirth. It makes no sense. Some claim the reason could be obesity and poverty, but average-size Black women and wealthy Black women are in just as much danger. Medical experts have their theories, but one stands out: According to our own government's research, many doctors do not respect a Black woman's pain. They do not listen to their patient's complaints and concerns. Therefore, they do not treat the symptoms that might lead to their death. Your mother was what they call a "near miss," a woman who barely survived complications of childbirth. That night I whispered to you both that your mother is the strongest woman in the world, and I meant it. I also told you that three other Black women, her doctors, were going to save her life, and they did.

It is also important to understand that peril lurks even in the places that we assume to be the safest, as well as in the hands of those who are supposed to protect us. Son, there are dangers happening in these streets.

While we see young Black men dying at the hands of the police today, I worry whether you will be safe walking in your own neighborhood or will be able to drive your own car without being scared for your life. Will we have clean air and water, or more wildfires and floods that threaten your and your children's lives? These questions have caused an unease in the world. The earth is sick as pestilence, fire, and odd weather envelop the globe, but I will not be just a passive observer, complaining from my couch. I refuse to wait and allow my son to inherit the same sick earth. But as much as I work for your freedom, the healing will not happen today.

*   *   *

I call you "Man Man" because it's just me and you, the only men in the house. And when I'm gone on yet another work venture, you know you need to be strong and be the head of the household, taking care of your two sisters and your mother. You are so protective of Sadie, your twin, and so loving to her. Sadie catches on to things quickly, but you, Stokely, you love to give hugs and kisses. I think you learned that early on, while we were in the hospital with your sister. You saw that your love and affection, your care for everyone, is an important contribution, and it is also what will make you a strong man.

There's a video of you blocking the door as I head out of the house. You can barely walk, but you're fierce in your resolve that I cannot leave you, leave my family. "No! No!" you insist, shaking your head, grabbing tightly onto my long legs. You stand there with a pacifier in your mouth, but your eyebrows are furrowed; your face is tight and manly. Your mother is in the background interpreting what she knows you'd say if you could. "You've been gone too much. I miss you. I need you."

Maybe the reason I taught you to be my little "Man Man" is the same reason you didn't want me to leave. I think even as a young child, you knew that there was a real and unspoken fear that every time a Black man goes outside, he might not come home. While you should have had the privilege of feeling secure that your daddy would always return, Black children and Black families have never had peace of mind. I pray for an America where Black boys and men can expect to be as safe as any white boy or man. But that day ain't here yet, and that causes me and your mother dread for you.

*   .   .   .*

There was this theory for a while among many African Americans, called double consciousness, regarding the ability to walk in different worlds—socially, at work, in different cultural atmospheres—and the pressures that come with that because you are Black. Today, in addition to that double consciousness, there is a double dose of anxiety. It's no longer just a matter of balancing how, when, and to whom we talk in the different social arenas, but a justifiable fear that we feel every day that we might be in danger for our lives.

We are seeing state-sanctioned violence, and violence from merely leaving your doorstep. Untimely death could also come from some of the preventable illnesses, such as a heart attack or prostate or colon cancer—Chadwick Boseman, an actor and hero who died much too early, comes to mind. When I think of all these illnesses that affect Black men at an early age, it scares me, but something else scares me even more. That's the fear of you, Stokely, my precious son, not coming home. Black parents like me only get a few years to try to sort through these fears before our Black boys are no longer truly babies. As I am sure you know by now, Black males don't get the virtue of still being considered a child when they reach the preteen and teenage years. The basic human consideration of being protected as a child is snatched away. As soon as a Black boy turns eight, nine, or ten years old, he is deemed to be a threatening man in the eyes of some.

There are many instances to prove my point, such as the white woman in New York City nicknamed Cornerstone Karen who falsely accused a little Black boy of touching her butt. She looked the nine-year-old child right in the eyes, in front of his mother, and told him, "I am calling the police on you." The boy, like any child would do, burst into tears, petrified of the cops, of being put in jail. That boy will never forget what happened to him. How could he? A video clip later showed that the boy's book bag accidentally touched the woman, but the little boy didn't notice because he was oblivious, focused on his mother.

There have also been numerous cases of little Black boys being suspended or expelled from school. A recent report on the California school system found that 20 percent of Black middle school boys were suspended at least once compared to 7 percent of white boys. Another study found that Black boys are eighteen times more likely than white boys to be treated as adult offenders. Sadly, Black girls are also treated like adults.

I recall watching a video on the news this year of a white police officer in Detroit laying his grown-ass body on top of a preteen Black girl as her mother and several other Black women held her hand, pleading for the police officer to get up off the child. That's where this type of double anxiety or double anxiousness I've been talking about comes to play. It has pushed me to do everything I can—mentally, physically, spiritually, and emotionally—to ensure I am as safe and as healthy as possible so I can take care of our family.

I only have until you are about the age of ten to try to make the changes that will ensure you are not prejudged and mistreated by people who diminish the humanity of being a Black man. I work hard every day to try to change the laws, the information, and the mindsets that justify the real fears associated with being a Black man in this country, fears that we cannot escape, regardless of how hard I try to raise you as a confident and wise Black child.

All Black Americans experience something called post-traumatic slave disorder, which is a palpable fear arising from a clear-eyed understanding of everything we've been through in this country over the past four hundred years. Knowing about this does not make us cowards; instead, it drives us in the face of whatever the hate or bigotry or xenophobia may be. We have utilized that fear to navigate obstacles, from slavery to Jim Crow, through the massacres that we've had in this country, from Tulsa to the nine murders in a Charleston church, to the one right here in Orangeburg, South Carolina, at which your granddaddy Cleveland was shot back in 1968. We're constantly met with that type of violence, that type of resistance, the slaughtering of our people of all ages in churches and businesses and schools—and still, we rise.

You come from people who persist at every opportunity; we get knocked down at nine, but we get back up by ten. That doesn't mean that we are removed from a healthy dose of apprehension about getting knocked down. Even if you see it coming, you can't stop the roller-coaster drop in your gut. Not a week goes by in which we're not feeling suffocated because these images of Black men being shot in the street force us to relive trauma.

Even though you and I didn't know George Floyd, we knew someone just like him in our own family. Our own reflections are played across TV screens and printed in newspapers (yes, we still had hard copies of those daily and weekly papers as I write this). Whether it's the gun violence of gangs or the state-

sanctioned violence of police, these travesties occur in such rapid succession that once you think we've turned a corner, you see another boy's picture, another name, another hashtag like #tamirrice or #michaelbrown. One of the things you must do is remember that, for some, this is just a story seen on a screen or read in a newspaper, but for you, son, these are stories of somebody's Black brother, husband, uncle, or nephew.

* * *

I've shared with you that anxiety runs in our family like a birthmark.

Your grandfather has it, your grandmother has it, and I have it. As a boy I was afraid of death, and I still am. So Stokely, I know that feeling you're feeling in your chest or your stomach; the anxiousness that you feel is normal. It's important that you do not let it eat at you but utilize that feeling to inspire you, to strengthen you to go out to be the change you wish to see in the world. You have to take the lessons learned from your grandfathers, and from all of those who have come before you, and know that you can't allow fear to paralyze you.

* * *

I've told you that your mother is the smartest, most beautiful, and most amazing woman in the world, and Sadie, your twin sister, is a superhero. As an infant, she had multiple surgeries and a scar to show for it. She was in the ICU on more than one occasion with feeding tubes keeping her alive. But since surviving that ordeal, Sadie has never fallen behind on anything and is now just as rough-and-tumble as you, her beloved twin brother. I think we can agree that is the true definition of bravery.

That brings me to something else. I haven't often felt hope-less as a grown man, but when your sister was sick, there were frequent moments when I felt like I had no control. The fear of losing someone that I loved so much became nearly insur-mountable. In situations like this, you must rely on your faith and on those who love you. Son, you are not in this world alone. And although things may get difficult or your fear may be all-consuming, Stokely, you must understand that prayer and family have helped our people survive more than four hundred years of struggles. So never lose your faith, son. And never for-get, we are here with you.

The Prescription

When I see Stokely, I can't help but smile. It's a love unlike any love one can find. You know, it's funny. I was watching Insta-gram Reels one day, and someone said that when you have a daughter, you will kill for her, and when you have a son, you'll die for him. And that's so true. With Stokely, I see my father in him, and I see my grandfather. I see Ellen's father in him too, in my boy's love of fishing and in the way he moves at his own pace, refusing to allow anything to speed him up. When I look in my son's eyes, I see pure joy and happiness just being in his father's arms. And I never want that to be ripped away from me because far too many of our peers are having to bury their children or other loved ones.

Stokely represents for me an entire generation that hope-fully one day will be able to free our world of the scourge of racism and bigotry and hate. Yes, that's a huge challenge to put on the shoulders of a young boy, but my generation is unfortunately going to leave that work incomplete.

*　*　*

I struggle, like most fathers and mothers of Black children, particularly Black boys, to explain the world that they're walking into. I struggle to explain how we were supposed to have a racial reckoning after Barack Obama or after George Floyd but that the racial reckoning never was and instead we experienced "whitelash."

I struggle to explain what's happening in the South, where the blatant disregard for examining and studying accurate portrayals of Black history has spread from Florida even to states like Arkansas. I struggle even more to explain what's happening in our courts and what's happening in the Lowcountry of South Carolina, where Black folk are fighting to hold on to their land, beautiful coastal land that they've owned since the Emancipation.

Every parent wants to give their kid a better world than the one they found, but we may be the first generation of parents who may not be able to do that. That's a tough pill to swallow. We must prepare young boys to continue and to take over this fight because we may be the first generation that must face the fact that the progress we thought we made is nil, and we're actually moving backward.

3

THE DAY OF THE LOCUST

There's no denying we're having a national (even international) moment.

As I look back on the years since George Floyd's death, this moment has taken on a haunting and—for me—biblical turn. Consider the locust outbreaks that struck East Africa with swarms stretching three times the size of New York City. Mosquitoes infected with the West Nile virus were detected in Los Angeles, while fires raged in the West and Canadian fires made the air from Maine to DC so red and cloudy that folk felt as if they were on Mars. In what might be the most biblical of scenes, red embers rained down in the ocean off Maui, setting the water ablaze. Another earthquake shook Haiti, and pediatric wards across the nation were filled with children sick from COVID-19.

Old Black folk, my mama included, believe that the book of Revelation is upon us, especially since we seem to be experiencing the ominous events the Bible declares will happen before the Second Coming of Christ. It all sounds very

familiar, especially if you're from generations of deeply spiritual folk, as I am.

I mentioned this to the Reverend Joseph Darby of Charleston, South Carolina. "That's hooey," he told me. A veteran
minister within the powerful African Methodist Episcopal
church, Reverend Darby is a great friend of mine and one of
those pastors willing to raise his voice and speak truth to
power to help the poor and downtrodden. The way he sees it,
all the strange things that are happening now are scientific
occurrences that have taken place in the past.

Still, some people have marked their doors with the cross,
a symbolic reimagining of what the Israelites did in Egypt to
avoid the ten plagues, as told in the book of Exodus.

Ellen and I never wanted COVID to enter our doors. Our
little Sadie is a liver transplant recipient, which means she's
on an anti-rejection medicine that suppresses her immune
system a little bit so that her liver isn't rejected by her body.
For me personally, it's not just the harm COVID could cause
my family, especially my immune-compromised little daughter, that causes me frustration, but it's also the political dialogue in this country, which is so infantile that we don't even
recognize that COVID has ripped the Band-Aid off the systemic inequities plaguing the Black community. You know,
I've always talked about growing up in a poor rural South
where water is tainted and the hospitals and grocery stores
have shuttered their doors, but COVID has exposed those
injustices through the catastrophic deaths and hospitaliza-
tions that have occurred, particularly to Black folk and Native Americans in this country.

During the early stages of the pandemic, Black Americans

were three times more likely than white people to die from COVID. A more astonishing statistic: 1 out of 420 Black people who were alive in January 2020 were dead three years later because of COVID.

When experts started examining COVID's wrath, the data indicated that where a person lived and worked could determine whether they live or die, which confirmed what many of us have been saying all along. However, it took a global pandemic and George Floyd's killing to awaken a government that had for centuries intentionally created laws that not only led to our deaths but also blocked African Americans from the mainstream channels of education, health care, and wealth.

In April 2021, Rochelle P. Walensky, then director of the Centers for Disease Control and Prevention, did something unprecedented. In a letter that was circulated throughout the media, she wrote, "The pandemic illuminated inequities that existed for generations and revealed for all America a known but unaddressed epidemic impacting public health: racism."

She said the disproportionate effect of the COVID-19 pandemic on Black and Brown people was proof that racism is an epidemic that negatively impacts the mental and physical health of millions, which in turn affects the entire nation.

The CDC specifically mentioned the words "implicit bias." But what does that mean? Implicit bias is a blind spot, a preconceived notion. My daddy used to say, "Even good white people have implicit bias." It's not racism, but it damn sure can lead to it—and racism can lead to death.

Walensky's comments were no doubt rare, but would we be having such a conversation if Hillary Clinton had become president? Weirdly, it was Donald Trump's presidency, along with his lies and racism, that forced us and the government to have an open conversation about the dangers of implicit bias and what we could do about it. My friend Garlin Gilchrist put it like this: "Research shows that the first step to eliminating the negative impact of implicit bias is to recognize that implicit bias exists."

And yet people still ask me, "Hey, why do you think so many African Americans are dying at higher rates from COVID?" People who ask the question don't even try to pull back the layers of the onion.

To say that COVID-related fatalities have touched my friend Garlin, a Detroit native and the lieutenant governor of Michigan, is a huge understatement. Garlin has known twenty-seven friends and relatives who contracted COVID and died.

"Very early on, I began to experience the phenomenon of getting text messages from my parents or my friends saying, 'Somebody you know got COVID; someone you know is in the hospital,'" he told me. "Then people I knew started passing. Most often they were Black."

Garlin and I are very similar. At thirty-eight, he's a millennial like me; we both love to hoop. He's a dark-skinned brother and tall like me, but at six-foot-eight, a few inches taller. He's always dressed impeccably in a suit. Although he wears glasses, he looks like he can give you thirty and ten on any given day on the basketball court. Though he's from the city, Detroit, and I'm from the country, the rural South, we both carry our hometowns on our shoulders.

"The first person was a friend of mine, a well-respected

guy in Detroit named Marlowe Stoudamire," Garlin told me. "Marlowe's dying was like, 'Oh my gosh, this is real.' Marlowe was in his mid- to late forties. He was a little overweight, but he was a relatively healthy guy. He died, and I was like, 'Damn, this is killing people who aren't sick.'"

After Marlowe, the deaths began to happen fast. It seemed every time he turned around, there was a new case and another death: "I made the choice early on, being that I'm the highest-ranking Black person ever to be elected in the history of the state of Michigan, to be public about the number of people who I personally knew of—friends, family, co-workers, former colleagues—who died of COVID. Early on it started out like this: I'd say, 'Hey, I know five friends, I know ten, I know fifteen, and now it's at twenty-seven.' I've chosen to do that because I wanted people to know that me as a policymaker and as a leader, that this is real for me. I'm not a disconnected, disinterested, dispassionate observer and decision-maker. I'm in it."

The Reverend Johnny Green, the associate pastor at the church Garlin grew up in, got COVID while he was officiating at a funeral. "Back when I was in college, our pastor who had been the pastor for a very long time died, and so Reverend Green held our church together for years. He grew up next door to my father. They both lived on the same street, on Thirty-Fifth Street in Detroit. My dad has known him his whole life. Reverend Green and his wife contracted COVID. They were both hospitalized, but she recovered. He did not. My dad will be sixty-five this year. Reverend Green was only sixty-four. He wasn't even an old man."

Several people who mentored Garlin began to die, one

after another. A former senator who advised him during Garlin's 2018 campaign died, and so did his childhood coach: "His name was Houston Martin, but we would call him Coach Punch. After the first AAU [Amateur Athletic Union] basketball season, when I was age nine, I was invited to come play in a parks and rec league in a suburb of Detroit. I was kind of a ringer. The coach for the parks and rec team was Punch. He had played ball earlier in life. He wasn't just an excellent player but had an excellent basketball mind. And he still had it. He could always shoot, and he just knew the game. I learned to play my best basketball for him. His son was on the team; in fact I had a group of friends that I got from Coach Punch, friends I had all the way from age ten to my final AAU season at age seventeen. That's when I played the best basketball of my life and almost got my way into a scholarship, even though I wasn't trying to get a basketball scholarship. I stayed in contact with Coach Punch and his son over the years."

Garlin learned Coach Punch was sick with COVID via Facebook. "He was only in his sixties, but he had serious diabetes. He was one of the people I talked about publicly during our weekly press conferences."

Much earlier, in April 2020, Garlin and his wife had to grieve a COVID victim who was special to both of them. Brenda Perryman was an educator and public figure in Michigan. Garlin and his wife had a friendship with her that was independent of their marriage.

"Bakari, that was a hard one for me," Garlin told me. "Ms. Perryman and my wife knew each other because Ms. Perryman taught in Southfield's [a suburb of Detroit] public schools. She used to also run a theater program at my wife's high school. My wife used to do a bunch of backstage stuff with the theater program. I met Ms. Perryman later, after college. She was a very public mentor. She also was known for hosting talk shows. When I ran for office, she had me on her TV show and a radio show a bunch of times. We just had a friendship over the years."

Perryman died about a month after the state saw its first COVID case, on March 10, 2020, which was the day of the presidential primary in Michigan. "We literally didn't even get to celebrate," Garlin said. "Kamala Harris announced her endorsement of former vice president Biden the night before in what was the final regular old-school-style political rally of the presidential campaign."

Garlin, Michigan's governor Gretchen Whitmer, Kamala Harris, Joe Biden, and Cory Booker were all at the Renaissance High School in Detroit. Garlin likes to say it was the last photograph to be seen for a very long time of Joe Biden and Kamala Harris together, smiling, and with no masks.

*　*　*

Sometimes my friends on the right, commenting on why COVID is killing Black and Brown people in such large numbers, will suggest that we must take individual responsibility. Others ask another bit of nonsense: Are Black people biologically predisposed to get COVID?

Dr. Ebony Hilton is a thirty-nine-year-old double-board anesthesiologist at the University of Virginia School of Medicine in Charlottesville, though she was born and raised in South Carolina. She is brilliant, beautiful, and unapologetically Black like me. She marched with Black Lives Matter in Charlottesville. And at the beginning of the pandemic, she sent a barrage of tweets to the CDC, urging them to reveal "who you're testing and who you are not." She provided COVID testing at shopping centers and churches, worried that minorities, who were most likely not getting tested at the time, could infect their communities.

When I asked if it was okay for her to be so outspoken, she said, "Honestly, I don't come from a medical family. I'm not married to any institution. I'm married to people. When you mention the demographic of a people who are dying more, how dare you tell me not to speak about Black people dying, when I'm talking about myself!"

Born and raised in a "small as hell" town named Little Africa, she also calls herself "country." Whereas Denmark is in the Lowcountry of South Carolina, Little Africa is in the upstate, near the foothills of the Blue Ridge mountains, cuddling up against its sleeker and more modern cousin, the city of Greenville.

Dr. Hilton has seen her share of severe COVID cases because, unfortunately, a good portion of people who are hospitalized with COVID end up needing to go into the ICU for long-term care. So the people Dr. Hilton sees in the ICU with COVID have had it for months. They're now on either just a ventilator or a heart-lung machine called an ECMO (extracorporeal membrane oxygenation) machine.

"If you're coming in and you're short of breath with COVID, we can give you those little cannula tubes in your nose to help give you oxygen," she said. "If that doesn't work, we then put you on a ventilator, where we place the breathing device in your mouth, and it goes down to your windpipe to help you breathe that way. And when that doesn't work, because your lungs are completely not working at all, then the next step is to put you on ECMO. You need ECMO when your heart or your lungs no longer work, and your body needs oxygen in order to live. We put a large catheter in your vein in your neck and in your legs; we take the blood out of your body and send it through a machine that basically has a pump to it that pumps the blood through another section of the machine that pushes oxygen into the blood and takes away your carbon dioxide from the blood, and then we put that blood back into the vein of your body."

I asked her the question I knew the answer to: Are Black people dying more from COVID than whites because of some kind of biological predisposition?

"Absolutely not!" she said, her southern twang rising in frustration. "For two reasons we had a problem. First, we must ask why are we more likely to be affected, and then why are we more likely to die? When everything shut down around the world, the reason Black and Brown people still were dying in such higher rates and whites were more largely protected was that the Black and Brown people were forced to go to work. If you look at the bulk of who is an essential worker, they were largely Black and Brown, and everyone else is working at home from Zoom."

As in many communities around the nation, Black people in Michigan were more likely to be those essential workers, toiling in a job that increased their risk of exposure to the virus. "Black folks are more likely to be working in a grocery store, be a bus driver, utility worker, a sanitation worker, to the nurse practitioner," my friend Garlin said. "They are overrepresented in these job functions, which were the ones that were critical in protecting and sustaining life during a pandemic. As a result of that, people doing these jobs were at a very high risk of exposure to the virus."

Another factor early in the pandemic—because the Trump administration was such a failure—was that nobody in the country had access to adequate COVID-19 testing. This led to medical professionals having to make the choice about who got a test and who didn't, and more often than not, Black Americans didn't. We have all these stories where Black people are telling us, "I went to the doctor, I went to the hospital, begging for tests. My uncle's sick, my mother is sick, I needed to get tested, and then being told no due to lack of supplies."

We can go much deeper into how implicit bias helped kill off African Americans during COVID. Let's talk about the vaccine rollout. The government tried to have a race-neutral policy, though the disease had racial health disparities, Dr. Hilton said. And that "makes it automatically pro-white in design."

For example, phase 1 was for health-care workers, of which over 60 percent are white. If you go down to phase 1B, officials then said, "'Let's focus on the age groups of seventy-five and older,'" she recalled, "but we know the life expectancy for Black people nationwide was only seventy-five."

"And so, you largely excluded Black people from that too," Hilton pointed out to me.

The government then said phase 1B can be for essential workers, but by April 2020, less than 50 percent of Black people had a job, so that excluded us too. And if you look at the people who work as a police officer, teacher, or firefighter, they're largely white.

The phase that Black people truly qualified for was that you had to have a preexisting condition like cancer or heart failure or renal failure.

"The government basically told Black people that despite being five times more likely to die from COVID, across all age groups, literally the only way you will fit in the early phases is you needed to have come into January 2020 with at least one of your organs already dead and gone," Dr. Hilton said. "You had to already have cancer or your heart, your kidneys, and your lungs not working before we consider you as a priority to get tested. That's the racism that we're dealing with."

* * *

Any discussion of high blood pressure, high cholesterol, or diabetes that does not talk about systemic racism is a nonstarter. Black people are four times less likely than white people to have a fully functioning grocery store in their neighborhood, and Black folk are twice as likely to not have a neighborhood hospital.

Being from Denmark, South Carolina, where there's only three stoplights and one grocery store, I've seen the effects a food desert can have on individuals and on an entire community. When you don't have access to fresh fruits and vegetables, you're more inclined to eat processed meat from the store or get a pound of sugar and a few packets of Kool-Aid. And because you're eating those processed meats, and you're drinking the Kool-Aid every week, you're more inclined to get high blood pressure or high cholesterol, and you're more inclined to get diabetes. Couple that with the fact that you live in a community where you're not drinking clean water, or maybe you live next to brown fields (lands that have been polluted) or you're inhaling unclean air—now you're more likely to get certain types of cancers, and you're predisposed to asthma or other respiratory illnesses.

Think of all this and then add the fact that rural hospitals are shutting down around the country. Dr. Hilton said, "And here's what people don't understand: we only have six thousand hospitals total in the United States of America. Only six thousand. That's not a lot. If you look at rural America, as far as rural community hospitals, there are only eighteen hundred."

She told me that in our home state of South Carolina, there's about eight counties without a single hospital. And then another fifteen of them only have hospitals with fewer than a hundred beds, all for acute-care patients. "Half of South Carolina literally is standing on a wish and a prayer," she said.

Now, overlay all of what I've been discussing with a pandemic, and it's no wonder Black folk are dying at higher rates. That's the context that's missing from the conversations. Because of those historic inequities—the lack of access to the health-care system, to health insurance, and to doctors—Black folk have had health conditions that have gone untreated for a very long time.

"And that's unfortunate," Dr. Hilton said. "If you get infected, and you have these comorbidities, because your organs have already been running on a treadmill for fifty years just trying to keep up, and now if I tell it to now sprint, it doesn't have any sprinting room," she said. "And that's what COVID makes your body feel like. It says, 'I know you need your lungs that have been subjected to toxins caused by the industrialization of your neighborhood, which has been polluting your lungs, and I know you've been dealing with that for decades, but now you have COVID.' Your lungs want to work, but they just don't have the functional reserve to work. That's why we were dying early on."

During those early days of COVID, Reverend Darby officiated over four funerals one right after another, including one for a mother and daughter. He's known sixteen people who have died of COVID, some of them very young and nearly all of them African American. "It's ravaging and frustrating," he told me. "I am not questioning God's will, but many of these people should still be alive."

* * *

We normally had someone to help us with our three-year-old twins, but when COVID hit we didn't want anybody outside of our home to come in. The reasoning was not only to protect us but also to protect them. The housekeeper who normally helps us, we had her stop. The babysitter who normally comes every day to assist us with the kids, we told her to stay at home.

Truth is, I was just as scared for Ellen as I was for the children. I didn't want to see her in the hospital again. I almost lost my wife after she gave birth to Stokely and Sadie. We were well aware before going into the hospital that our health-care delivery system does not respect the pain that Black folk go through, that our pain is not looked at with the same urgency as that of white folk in this country, which is why, as I mentioned earlier, we specifically made sure the doctors who operated on my wife looked like Ellen. Because of them, Ellen is here with me today, but not everyone is as lucky as we are.

In 2020, Susan Moore, a fifty-two-year-old Black doctor suffering from COVID-19 at Indiana University Health North, took to Facebook to complain about the treatment she was receiving from her doctor. Lying in the hospital bed, connected to a tube, she said her neck was in severe pain, but her doctor didn't believe her and balked at her request for pain medicine and a CT scan. Only after tests showed inflammation in her neck and chest, according to news accounts, did she get the medicine and the scan. Struggling to speak, Dr. Moore said in the viral video, "He treated me like a drug addict. He knew I was a physician. I've never taken narcotics."

Moore was a doctor and also a human, which makes her story all the more tragic. "I put forth and I maintain if I were white, I wouldn't have to go through that," she said. "This is how Black people get killed, when you send them home and they don't know how to fight for themselves."

After Moore was eventually sent home, she was readmitted to another hospital, but her health only deteriorated. She died less than two weeks after posting to Facebook.

After her death, Indiana University Health formed an outside panel made up of six medical experts, four of them Black, to look into Moore's death, according to the *Indianapolis Star*. The panel found that Moore's death wasn't caused by the treatment she received from the hospital. However, the report claimed that Moore did suffer from "a lack of cultural competence" on the part of those who treated her. The IU Health president said in a statement that the hospital would have to do more "to address implicit racial bias," add more diversity training, and find ways to give all patients a voice.

*   *   *

We thought we were being extremely vigilant, but COVID came to our home anyway. During the first part of the pandemic, Ms. Ruby, Ellen's eighty-year-old mother, popped over to the house as she often does. Normally healthy (she swims every single morning at the YMCA), Ms. Ruby was coughing and hacking.

This was in October 2020.

I remember she came to the house on a Wednesday. Ellen's family is large and very close. Since her father's death nearly two years before, Ellen makes sure she calls her mother in the morning and before she goes to bed, but that day she was worried about Sadie.

She said, "Mom, you're going to have to leave my house. You are coughing way too much." Sure enough, two days later, Ms. Ruby got diagnosed as having COVID. We were scared as hell because she's diabetic. We were also very scared for Sadie, but for the grace of God we didn't get it. Ms. Ruby said, "I'll be just fine," and she was. She had her twenty-six-year-old granddaughter living with her, who was also diagnosed. They quarantined together and took care of each other.

*   *   *

The private school that Kai, our fifteen-year-old daughter, attends opened in August 2020. The administration allowed their one thousand students to decide whether they wanted to attend school in person or go virtual. They even had a few weeks to decide. Kai, who was entering her sophomore year, was extremely excited to see her friends and be in school after months of being isolated in the house. But when she returned, the school she knew was a very different place. Everyone had to wear a mask and sit six feet apart in class, which sometimes made it hard for students to hear each other. During lunch, they were mandated to sit outside with the same four students. Each student had to scan a barcode on the table to alert the school that they were sitting with their assigned group.

School had become a weird and unusual place for Kai and her classmates, especially when they got the dreaded news that they might have been exposed to COVID. Once someone contracted the virus, the contact tracing began: the school nurses visited classrooms with a long-ass measurement tape, computing the seating distances. Kai was in art class, her last class of the day, when she got a text from Ellen.

"I need to come and get you. Now," Ellen wrote.

"Why?" Kai texted back.

"You've been contact-traced."

"What?" Kai said. "What if I have COVID?"

When Kai described recently how she felt that day, I can still hear the frustration in her voice. "It's terrifying and it's sad because I couldn't control not going home or preventing myself from getting contact-traced. . . . I just went to the office, where there were other students who had to leave too. They were crying; it was really sad the first time."

Unfortunately, it happened again. She was especially upset because it meant she couldn't attend volleyball practice. That's when Kai decided to go virtual until after Thanksgiving.

In February 2021, Ellen drove Kai to Tennessee for a recreational volleyball game while I stayed with the twins. I like to think of these road trips as a little mini vacation for my supportive wife, who not only cares for our kids when I'm away for work but also runs her own business. While they were in Tennessee, Kai noticed that one of her teammates was showing signs of COVID: she had a headache; she was nauseous and coughing. The student was diagnosed with COVID within a week. Ellen was worried because we had an immune-compromised child in the home, so she made plans to get rapid tests for us all. That's when Kai started feeling sick.

"I got COVID! I just know it," she said, even before she got tested.

We needed to know pretty fast whether anyone had contracted the virus.

By the grace of God, none of us got sick except Kai, who we knew was old enough to fend for herself. Because of Sadie, we told Kai she had to stay in her room for fourteen days. We'd take food on paper plates to her door. Ellen would slide the food into Kai's room and wear gloves to bring Kai a trash bag for her garbage. Kai, who is in love with Sadie and didn't want her sister harmed, would wear gloves and a mask to bring the plate back outside her bedroom door.

One day, a strange thing happened. Kai was eating breakfast and called out, "I can't taste anything."

Ellen assured her it was just allergies.

"No, I'm serious. . . . I can't taste!" she called out.

Once Kai lit a candle in her room but couldn't smell it, we knew she had lost both smell and taste. She couldn't eat foods with specific textures, like eggs. All she wanted to eat was pasta (her favorite food), but we made sure she also had soup and salads.

We were very careful about having her come downstairs. Although she didn't have a fever, she was very tired and achy, almost like she had the flu. We were happy she didn't have to be hospitalized, but we were still cautious. When individuals get COVID, particularly young people, we still don't know the lasting effects. Kai had to go to the cardiologist to be cleared to play volleyball because COVID can cause myocarditis or inflammation of the heart muscles. Although we're very prayerful and she's fine now, we still feel angst when young people contract COVID. We know children do not have immunity as we initially thought, and they are not recovering as quickly as we thought they would, especially with the delta variant.

The Prescription

If we're going to talk about how COVID impacted Black people living in cities and small towns and how we can fix things, it would be irresponsible not to include Detroit in that analysis. Detroit, which is 79 percent Black, still retains the title of the Blackest major city in the country. Michigan is one of the states that was hit hardest by the pandemic. While Black people make up only 14 percent of the state's population, we accounted for 40 percent of the COVID cases. The reason people nationally know who Governor Gretchen Whitmer is, even before she was considered by Joe Biden as a possible running mate, is that she was on TV going off about COVID-19 because it was hitting Michigan so hard.

The state was one of the first to set up a task force not only to look at the role that medical bias had played in treatment decisions and diagnoses but also to come up with solutions: "We were having a disproportionate number of people of color being untreated, which also led to more severe outcomes and more mortality," Garlin said. "Our chief medical executive is a Black woman. One of the first interventions of the task force was for her to write a letter to every medical professional in the state of Michigan, explaining that implicit medical bias has a potential to cause poor outcomes during the pandemic, and overall."

Not everyone in Michigan was happy to get that letter, but the truth hurts. The state made another bold move. As part of the medical licensing process in Michigan, medical professionals are now required to undergo implicit bias training.

Garlin headed the Coronavirus Task Force on Racial Disparities, which sought to set up systems to flatten the African American deaths by (1) increasing transparency in reporting data showing racial impact of the virus, (2) reducing medical bias in treatment and testing, (3) mitigating environmental factors, and (4) supporting long-term economic recovery systems.

"We got right to work," Garlin said. And it seemed to have paid off. Black people accounted for 41 percent of the COVID deaths in Michigan early on, but that number decreased to 8 percent in 2021.

Nationally, Black and Latino numbers had kept steady, but the number of white deaths surged. Every month, 15,000 white Americans were dying, but after Thanksgiving 2020, it jumped to 27,000, according to a 2021 Research Lab project by American Public Media. After Christmas, it jumped to 42,000 a month, and after New Year's white deaths rose to 47,000. And 58,475 white Americans died between February 2 and March 1. If you look at that breakdown for Blacks and Latinos, there was only a small increase.

"The rise in white deaths from COVID, however, was strictly because of behavior choices," Dr. Hilton said. "It's not because Black people are dying less, it's because white people are dying more. They took off their masks, they refused to follow basic public health measures, and it's killing them," Hilton said. "With the delta variant rise, which is creaming the South and Midwest, we have the potential to see where the racial disparity gets completely erased, because white people are going to be dying at such high rates. And that is also a tragedy."

. . .

So, what else do we do? How can we wipe out the racial disparities the right way? Dr. Hilton and her colleagues wrote a memo to the Congressional Black Caucus suggesting a federal Department of Equity. "Just like we have a Department of Transportation, Department of Education, HHS, we need a Department of Equity, where literally every policy that comes out of each of those other departments has to go through an independent investigation by this entity to say, 'Is this thing rooted in equity?'" Dr. Hilton said. She hasn't heard from the Black Caucus yet.

For me, the prescription is a little different. I'm not certain that we've addressed the real issue in this country when it comes to COVID, which is more than wearing a mask or getting a shot and washing your hands. It's about going in and reimagining what these poor Black and Brown communities that have been left behind should really look like. COVID has not only killed thousands of Black people, but it has massacred our small businesses, which have been our lifeline for decades. I like to use the word "reimagine" because it's important as we rebuild these communities to envision them with the necessities, like grocery stores and hospitals, that every American should be afforded.

We also have to consider the environmental injustices that are ravaging our communities and causing cancers and that we have simply not addressed yet. So yes, COVID has caused a great deal of anxiety but even more frustration. If we don't fix these inequities, and soon, at the end of the day, when this virus is fully under control and we're all outside playing football games and barbecuing, Black people will still be dying.

4

THE GREAT RETURN

Ellen and I were just meant to connect. Black folk. Smart folk. Southern church folk, raised in families where worship was as critical as breathing.

When I was a very young boy, my family would attend two churches every Sunday in Denmark, South Carolina: a Baptist one and an Episcopalian one, where I was an acolyte just like my father forty years earlier. I helped with all the funerals, I finished the wine, I prepared the incense, I lit the candles, and I took up the offering. We were in Bible study on Wednesdays, and we had choir practice too. That was on Thursday and Friday, and then my mother prepared the programs for the church and helped with the flowers on Sunday.

It felt like we lived in the church back then. And after all that has happened—from struggles with Sadie's health to the horror COVID brought to the world to the tragic deaths of unarmed Black men in the streets—I longed to find comfort in the church again during the pandemic, but of course that was not to be. I love God, but I was not going to put my family in jeopardy. I don't think that there's anywhere in the scripture that says "Thy must be stupid."

Recently, I've noticed that church people have been talking about "the return" to the physical church, but are we sure what we will be returning to? In my childhood, the church was always there for us, playing various roles and serving as a voice for the voiceless. It was a sacred place that fed us spiritually, providing the sustenance and the strength to help us move forward. It was also an institution that was deeply involved in our community. These days, people fear that COVID has transformed the Black church forever, but in truth the church has been moving away from being active in our communities for some time.

As a justice-seeking millennial, I believe Black folk need our churches to step up now more than ever. As we emerge from the pandemic, still grieving the losses from COVID and the deaths of innocent Black men and women like George Floyd, Breonna Taylor, and Ahmaud Arbery at the hands of police, we need the Black church to return to its roots, to be a place where we can again be uplifted politically, a place that uses its credibility to fight for policy changes.

But what has the Black church done for us lately? Why are so many churches only ministering on Sunday, leaving their communities without a church presence from Monday through Saturday? Where were Black ministers during the demonstrations after George Floyd's murder?

Of course, my critique is all a generalization, but it's also an expectation. I believe that any challenge or critique comes from a place of love. I want to be a part of a church family that is spiritual and religious and also has the level of community engagement and activism that I remember.

* * *

I grew up hearing firsthand about the role of the church during the civil rights movement. The Reverend Martin Luther King became the face of the movement, as he traveled 6 million miles and gave twenty-five hundred speeches at churches, community centers, rallies, and union halls from 1957 to 1965.

Meanwhile, Uncle Stokely talked my father into quitting Howard University to join the movement full-time. When Dad and hundreds of other workers and volunteers needed to find meeting space in Georgia or Mississippi, they turned to the church for help. As Dad moved through the dangerous deep South, the church was often a refuge, a place for the young demonstrators and activists to organize and congregate. The situation was different in the very hot summer of 2020. As my older brother, Lumumba, a Gen X minister, said, "There were church people running away from Black Lives Matter. They wanted to support them, but there were church folk who didn't want to be associated with them. They made it a point to say, 'We're not Black Lives Matter, but we believe that Black lives do matter.'"

To be fair, Black ministers like T. D. Jakes did speak out against the police killings of innocent Black men, and some Black ministers, such as Rev. William Barber, even stood on the front lines during demonstrations after George Floyd's death. But was it enough?

*   *   *

Long before the 1950s and '60s, Christianity and politics were interconnected. The church was key to survival during enslavement. Black folk gathered to worship at least as early as the 1700s, and the First African Baptist Church was formally established in Savannah, Georgia, in 1777. As historian Henry Louis Gates Jr. said, "One of the greatest achievements in the long history of civilization, as far as I am concerned, is the extraordinary resilience of the African American community under slavery, through the sheer will and determination of these men and women to live to see another day, to thrive."

While most white slaveholders tried to use Christianity, among other means, to keep their human property in their place, our ancestors took the religion of the oppressor and made it their own by refashioning stories like Moses delivering the Israelites from the bondage of Pharaoh to reflect their shared circumstances. From the spirituals and biblical stories, our ancestors discovered strength and hope that God would make a way out of no way. Think about this: fifty different African ethnicity groups were a part of the Middle Passage, packed into ships that sailed to North America, which meant these families eventually had to forge themselves into one group. The Black church undoubtedly served as a laboratory for the creation of Black culture.

Frederick Douglass grounded his movement for Black emancipation on the bedrock of Christian faith, and he spoke repeatedly at Black churches. In fact, he was licensed to preach by a congregation at the AME Zion Church in New Bedford, Massachusetts.

W. E. B. Du Bois's earliest works focused on Black churches, which he saw as the center of the Black community at the turn of the twentieth century. Even Marcus Garvey, who wasn't a churchgoer, called for the creation of an independent national church for African Americans.

It's likely the Civil Rights Act of 1964, and the Voting Rights Act of 1965, would never have become established law without the Black church. And yet, the great and late historian Manning Marable said something profound and unfortunately quite true. He explained that while Black churches had the institutional resources and the ability to fund long-term protest, and they did, most Black ministers during the civil rights era stood on the sidelines and didn't participate in the civil disobedience or the campaigns of Dr. Martin Luther King. For example, he said only about twenty-five to thirty-five of the two hundred churches in the city of Birmingham participated in the voting and anti-segregation campaigns in that city.

As my father and the other organizers discovered during the Montgomery bus boycott and when they stopped in southern states such as Georgia, the marriage between religion and politics could be a tense one. The organizers had to call mass meetings to inform people about what was going on; they also needed to find people involved with the movement who could talk about their experience to other locals, including the risks and the sacrifices that had to be made.

My dad said when they went into communities like Albany, Georgia, they recognized that they had to organize the community, especially those willing to sit down in order for minorities to stand up. Interestingly, Daddy said the people who became part of organizing in the movement were primarily women.

"In the effort to organize, we needed to reach out to the dispossessed," he said. "We organized the people who were shut out and were never considered to be important figures in the movement, and in many instances that happened to be women."

If my dad and other activists and volunteers wanted to hold a mass meeting in a church, the workers and volunteers had to get permission from the ministers, which wasn't always an easy thing to do. "We couldn't do it in some instances because the preacher looked at us as outsiders creating a disturbance, and that's likely the rationale for some churches not being involved," Daddy said. "But fortunately for us, the church, especially the Black church, had those women's organizations, and so we could get women to go in and apply the pressure."

Dad says even when people talk about student involvement in the movement, they leave out the Black women. Ella Baker, who inspired my father, Uncle Stokely, and other young people to create the Student Nonviolent Coordinating Committee, has great credentials for being a civil rights hero, but she was marginalized because there was an effort in the movement to feature the male figures as the most dominant and the most progressive.

The simple truth is that the men at that time, especially the ministers, didn't want to hear about women being in the pulpit. They were clearly chauvinist.

*　　*　　*

To be fair, Black ministers had good reason to be wary about helping the activists during the '60s. Dad was in Mississippi in the summer of 1964 as one of hundreds of Freedom workers who arrived in the state as part of the Mississippi Summer Project, also known as Freedom Summer. The project was launched in June of that year to register African American voters in the state.

Dad was based in Holly Springs, where workers helped organize voter registration but also opened freedom schools and freedom libraries in nine counties. Despite all the good they were doing, it was a terrifying and bloody ten weeks. White residents resented all the outsiders coming into the state. Churches were being set on fire to scare local African Americans and prevent them from registering to vote. During that summer, my father remembers dozens of Black churches being destroyed in Mississippi alone.

Being the cause of a church burning or someone's death weighed on the young people's hearts and minds. After each arson, the workers would visit the site of the church, investigating the tragedy and raising money to rebuild. This, sadly, was why James Chaney, Andrew Goodman, and Michael Schwerner had returned to Philadelphia, Mississippi.

* * *

My father says the recent tragic deaths of so many Black victims of police violence, and the demonstrations and protests that followed, remind him of the turmoil of the 1960s. "It's like we're reliving it," he says.

It's all just worn us out, which is why the Black church must once again be a place not just of spiritual and religious sustenance but also where we can take action against injustices. It must be a place where we can not only show up but also organize. How do we bring the church back to its roots? That's going to be a challenge. But one place to look for the answers is in my favorite scripture: "Faith without works is dead" (adopted from James 1:17). This scripture from the book of James perfectly explains the crossroads the Black church finds itself in right now: Should the church be all faith or a combination of faith and work?

This scripture helps us understand that words like "love" and "justice" and "truth" are verbs: we have to give them life; we have to breathe into them meaning. We have to take action to achieve and accomplish all of those things.

The standard is not the same as it used to be, Rev. Joseph Darby explained to me. "When the Bible says faith without works is dead, it means that faith without something connected to it means that the faith is really dead. As far as the works, it's not just saying be busy; it's saying be busy doing the right thing, like fighting for justice."

A 2021 study by the Barna Group, a research company based in California, found that Black Americans want and need the church to return to its activist roots. The study found that 73 percent of Black adults (and 75 percent of Black churchgoers) felt politically disempowered compared to 1996, when only 61 percent of Black adults felt politically powerless. What's particularly interesting is that the study also showed that most Black people not only looked to the church for comfort but also expected the church to be politically astute. A total of 71 percent of the Black population polled in 2020 (and 79 percent of churchgoers) said that spiritual and social issues should be the top priorities of the church. A mere 6 percent of Black adults (and 4 percent of Black churchgoers) believed the church should be "purely spiritual." One in four Black adults, or 23 percent, believed the church should focus on social justice issues only.

*   *   *

Reverend Darby said the doctrine used to be about the community, giving to the poor, and equality, rather than only about blessings and faith:

> When I was growing up, church was the center of community and necessity because there was still segregation and there was no other place you could go. And so, the church became the place to worship, became the place of all-day Sunday socialization, became the place where the needs of the people in the community were cared for. It became the tip of the spear for the civil rights movement; the church became all of that. There's been a couple of years of evolution since then. After the sixties, the Black church—along with the rest of America, I think—made the mistake of thinking that civil rights laws meant that you would overcome, and didn't understand that laws can't change hearts.

Darby observed that there was gradually less emphasis on the church as a central place of activity and more as a place that you go on Sunday. And in most recent years, there's been an inordinate emphasis on praise at the expense of social activism.

"One of the things that I throw into a sermon is that there's too many churches all shouting but no service. That's the problem," Darby said. "You have the white churches thinking their conscience is clear because if you talk about civil rights, talk about advocacy, they say, 'It's over. We give to the poor. We send money to Africa. We have food kitchens.'"

All those acts are wonderful, but they're not enough. And the Black churches, Reverend Darby said, can't stop doing what needs to be done and still say, "We've done our bit."

To drive his point, he told me, "Bakari, Dr. Martin Luther King, the pastor, would have had a soup kitchen. King, the civil rights leader, would have asked, 'Why is there a need for a soup kitchen in the richest country in the world?'"

*   *   *

I have mentioned that my maternal grandfather was the Reverend E. W. Williamson, a prominent member of the National Baptist Convention, which for a long time was the largest Black-owned business in the country and the largest denomination for Black people. The National Baptist Convention made social justice a critical part of Christian faith and the civil rights platform. They were the movement. Churches sang about social justice, about moving forward and getting through.

My grandfather always wanted to look the part. What I mean is he always wanted to have the appearance of being a leader. He'd even cut the grass in dress pants and dress shoes. When he went to the grocery store, he had to get dressed to the nines. When he walked in the room, he commanded it. That was who he was, but he also fought injustices by helping the civil rights activists of the day. When my grandfather was coming up as a Baptist pastor, he didn't care if he had one person or five hundred people in his church. Rather, his success was all about how he impacted the local community. Ministers like my grandfather partnered with the civil rights movement; they allowed people to come into their churches to preach and into their homes.

Reverend Darby is cut from the same cloth as my grandfather; ministers like Darby are dubbed "old-school" these days because they are always fighting for a cause, always searching for justice. In other words, he is my kind of minister.

Born in Columbia, South Carolina, in 1951, Darby is the senior pastor of Nichols Chapel in Charleston. The church is named after Bill Ruffin Nichols who, sometime after the Civil War, rebuilt Mother Emanuel AME Church after it was burned down by local racists. Nearly a century later, the Mother Emanuel was the site of a massacre in 2015 when Dylann Roof, a young white supremacist, walked into the church during Bible study. An hour later, he shot and killed nine Black parishioners, including the pastor and my good friend, Clementa Pinckney.

Like Clem, Reverend Darby has held top positions in the powerful AME church system, but he's known for his activism in Charleston. "Generally, I have a big mouth, and I'm fairly prolific when it comes to opinion columns in the paper," Reverend Darby told me. "You got some pastors who can shout all day long in church—they have what I call the shout-itis—but when it comes to speaking truth to power, some of them won't do it because they fear that they might fall out of the graces of those in power who might control funds for the community. But see, you can't bark while you are chewing on a bone, and too many of my colleagues like to chew on a bone instead of barking."

These same ministers tell Reverend Darby, "You must be crazy writing all that stuff in the newspaper." Still others say, "He's good, but he's old-school. I don't want to hear what he has to say. It's going to take too long. I want to hear about blessings."

* * *

How did we go from decades of activism to focusing purely on our own blessings and being highly favored? My brother, Lumumba, has been critical of the church in general and the Black church in particular for a while now. He believes the change happened in the early '90s, during the beginning of the prosperity preaching era.

"That's when you had the emergence of the evangelical," Lumumba said. "In walked Kenneth Copeland, a white pastor who developed this huge following of people. He preached at his church, but where he really made his name was when he traveled and preached everywhere else."

Kenneth Copeland was very intentional with his actions. First, he developed this biblical message around prosperity and blessings. He was like, "open up the windows of heaven, and a car will drop out of the sky," Lumumba said. Copeland emphasized drawing out these blessings by claiming there's nothing wrong with having money.

"The second part is, he 'fathered' a lot of young African American pastors," Lumumba explained. "In the Christian faith, what that means is, he basically said, 'I'm going to help you, help you grow your church, help you finance, help you strategize, and I am your spiritual father.' A lot of these young pastors adopted that same message. In the Black community, that message of money and blessings overtook Black churches."

"Don't block your blessing" is still a popular phrase, as is "I'm blessed and highly favored."

The result was the rise of something we'd never seen before: the Black megachurch. Lumumba observed that we began to see pastors like Bishop Eddie Long and Creflo Dollar, all of them trained by Copeland. "In the LA area alone, you could go from churches of five hundred people to one thousand people to maybe a couple of thousand to churches of twenty thousand people." Then there were these huge budgets, Rolls Royces, and airplanes.

"It almost desensitized the church," Lumumba continued. "And it made the standard to be that if you're not shepherding a whole lot of people to make a whole lot of money, you're not successful. What that has ultimately done is watered down the impact of the church in the local community and disappointed many churchgoers who lost faith in church leaders."

The New Normal?

Back in April 2020, more than a month before George Floyd's violent death, the *Washington Post* said up to thirty bishops and prominent clergy within the Church of God in Christ, the largest African American Pentecostal denomination, had died or were dying of COVID. Health officials claimed that funerals and conferences held within the denomination led to the deaths. Other media stories looked at the deaths of local Black and white church leaders in cities across the nation.

Now consider the tens of thousands of Black parishioners who died of COVID and won't be sitting in their favorite church pews anymore. This begs the question: What will the Black church look like after the so-called great return?

From the deacons who basically run the church, to the ushers who troubleshoot problems and guide us to our seats, to the choir directors who masterfully provide us with music, the Black church has offered parishioners the leadership positions they often cannot find in white America. However, when COVID forced the church to close its doors, it also transformed the way we worship: ministers who were energized by large crowds of people found themselves preaching to an audience they couldn't see.

While it was hard to watch a seventy-five-year-old African American minister try to hold an internet church service, retired parishioners discovered a new and convenient way of worshipping: they could remain in the comfort of their homes but also chat with the minister in real time. Some Black professionals found virtual churches were too closely akin to Zoom meetings for work, so they just held off and binged them like a Hulu series.

Lumumba noticed that white churches were a little more prepared for virtual church, while most of the Black churches didn't have the technology. "They didn't focus on the production aspect of the church," he said. "So some ministers had to tell everybody, 'Go home. We don't have service.' And oh, by the way, there's no way to generate revenue."

You couldn't just do a basic church service, run a couple of cameras, and call it a day. To grab people, you had to have a full production. If that didn't happen, ministers learned, church folk will leave you and start watching a church with a real video production.

"The church I went to in Atlanta, it took them six months to figure out how to do a live service," my brother recalled. "They were recording videos and then uploading it for months only to people that logged in with a password."

Black churches just could not figure it out, and so they struggled. "A lot of churches struggled because that infrastructure just wasn't there," my brother explained. "At the end of the day, you cannot survive like that."

Many of Lumumba's friends, who are Black pastors, are no longer pastoring after COVID. They lost everything—their flock, their church, and the funds to keep the church open—and they quit. In the Black church, COVID was devastating. These ministers tried to do all the right things, and they had to shut their doors.

"The ones that didn't are the ones like in North Carolina, where you saw this little, small denomination, I don't even know what they're called, but they decided to go around to different churches with their 'bishop' and have services," Lumumba said. "At the beginning they were bringing older people from nursing homes to the church. They had a service in North Carolina, and almost everybody, including the pastor, got COVID. People died, but I know what the church was attempting to do. They were trying to be creative; in their mind, they were trying to stay afloat."

While it has been hard for the Black church to survive as we get through COVID, the church will not sink. It has had many evolutions through the centuries. Will the church be the same after COVID? Most likely not, but it will survive.

When you have to close the church doors and you're not able to put those butts in the seats, it's very difficult from a practical standpoint to continue to operate. Still, the threat to the church began long before the pandemic.

The Prescription

Dr. Ebony Hilton believes the church could have done a better job of discouraging Black parishioners from coming to church during COVID and a better job encouraging people to get vaccinated. The key, she explained to me, is not to try to "pray it away," but to use the biblical word to illustrate what is going on. "I was raised Baptist, and I very much am a Christian," Dr. Hilton said.

When I think about God, I think energy, everything is connected. And so, I don't understand people who look at religion and science as two separate things. Especially from a religious standpoint, if you're going to say that God is the Alpha and Omega, that he's the creator of all, then you can't pick and choose what "all" is. Right? We can't say in seven days he created everything, including you and me, and not say that he also had a hand in knowing what this pandemic will look like. I think we're supposed to use the Bible as a road map of how to respond because it's not like this is something new. We had the pandemic of 1918. Got one in 2019. And we're going to have to learn from those events or keep making the same mistakes.

She suggested that if ministers are going to say God created all things, then include vaccines. "We should have been
using the stories of the Bible to highlight the importance of
listening and watching for the times of trouble. Instead of
preaching, 'Oh, just trust God, and we're just going to still
convene,' they should have been preaching the story of Noah
and the Ark and how do we make sure we're keeping our people safe?"

In the church's defense, however, Hilton said there were a
lot of Black churches that did try to get the message out. And
if it wasn't for the Black church helping organize the vaccine
drives and the mobile clinics that had to be set up in Black
communities, in barbershops and other places, we wouldn't
have as many people vaccinated as we have today.

* * *

No one can deny that the Black church was so central to the
recent Georgia political victories that Republicans in the
state legislature are now trying to end Sunday voting. Voters were mobilized by people like Stacey Abrams, Helen Butler, and LaTosha Brown, but Georgia's Black church "souls to
polls" movement also contributed to Black voters making up
a third of Georgia's total electorate population and being responsible for nearly half of Georgia's total electorate growth
from 2000 to 2019, according to the Pew Research Center.

Across the nation, progressive reforms are taking place in
some Black churches—hiring female ministers, embracing
LGBTQ+ members—but the rise of voter suppression and of
killings of innocent Black people by police calls for the faith-
based activism of the past. As I have already mentioned, there

have always been those who believe there is no place for faith-based organizing in the church, even during the civil rights movement. But our present-day problems have allowed us to view history with kinder, gentler eyes, and so we must accept those lessons learned and implement them in the future of the church so we can make it what it once was.

Whether or not we've been decimated by COVID or by natural events like hurricanes or global warming, we have to have a church that's more than a place to refill our hope. We need a place where we can learn how to apply for federal grants and assistance programs to rebuild our communities, where we can drop our kids off for school, and where we can organize precinct meetings and launch campaigns for political office.

I also want the church to be an organization that goes out and feeds the hungry. We need our churches to be all of these things, as they used to be in the past. It's a lot to ask, but if the church won't do it for our people, who will?

5

WHITE TERROR, PART 1

Mississippi, 1964

I was on a podcast shortly after my breakdown on CNN was televised all over the world. The Charlotte, North Carolina–based host said to me, "You were on CNN, talking about these protests that are going on around the country, and you broke down and you said something in your pain that I think should resonate with everybody and make them think about the impact of systemic racism. You said, 'I get so tired. We have Black children. I have a fifteen-year-old daughter. What do I tell her? I'm raising a son. I have no idea what to tell him. It's hard being Black in this country when your life is not valued.' What *do* you tell your daughter, because she's the oldest?"

I responded with something like this: I tell my daughter that when the police are behind you, make sure you go to a brightly lit area. I tell her that whatever you do, do not stop on the side of the road. Just head to the gas station and dial 911.

Let the operator know that you are being followed by a police officer and you're going to the nearest gas station. I tell her to make sure that you don't back-talk or raise your voice, and I explain that we will fight these battles in court.

What most people listening that day didn't know is that the survival hacks that I teach my daughter and will teach the twins one day are the same tips Dad taught to me. The difference is that he learned them back in 1964 when he was trying not only to fight against racism but also to survive white terrorism in the hot Delta summer.

* * *

During the civil rights struggles of 1964, around thirty-five Black churches were burned down, shot up, or blown to pieces in Mississippi alone. My father was there, as was Uncle Stokely, who had encouraged Dad to drop out of Howard University and be a full-time activist with the Student Nonviolent Coordinating Committee. Dad agreed, partially because he needed to be part of the movement but also because he wanted to get away from my granddad, who desperately needed him home safe in Denmark, South Carolina.

But what Dad experienced that year in the Delta was even worse than the burning of dozens of churches. Dad described that hot summer of 1964, Freedom Summer, as the worst time of his life. In fact, when Dad described the nights that he and others went looking for the three missing activists (Andrew Goodman, James Chaney, and Michael Schwerner), I could feel the fear in my own bones. That summer "was the longest nightmare I have ever had," Dad wrote in his memoir eight years after all that horror. "I was nineteen years old, a man-child immersed in the seething core of the long hot summer."

Recently, my father provided more context about that summer. "As seventeen-, eighteen-, and nineteen-year-olds, we had to come to grips that we were putting the community in harm's way. And when we asked ourselves the question if we were responsible for the Black Mississippians we were trying to register to vote, you had to be in the right mindset to analyze what it was that you were doing, and how basic and necessary the change was, in order for us to make those decisions and to keep trucking."

Most of the SNCC workers like my father, and the hundreds of white Ivy League students they recruited to help register poor Black Mississippi residents to vote, left with their lives, but as Dad said, "None of us escaped without terrible scars." The wounds, that post-traumatic stress, remains deep inside him today and will be with him for the rest of his life.

*   *   *

Although 207,000 Black people were eligible to vote in Mississippi, only 6 percent were registered. SNCC's job was not only to get them registered but to turn them into leaders.

African Americans were the majority in many counties, which is why racist systems were set up in Mississippi in the first place, to keep Black people from the polls. Voting officials would require Black residents to guess how many jelly beans were in a jar in order to register. Black teachers and professors were told they didn't pass the simple required reading test.

During Freedom Summer, there were one thousand arrests, dozens of church bombings, thirty homes and buildings
burned, six murders, and eighty-something beatings. But that
doesn't describe the hell the locals dealt with on a daily basis.

"We knew there were going to be adverse consequences,"
Dad said. He and his colleagues all knew something could
and likely would pop as a result of the registration drive:
Black Mississippians could be killed. Overnight, they could
lose their jobs as bus drivers or workers on a plantation.
Their children could be kicked out of school, and the local
government could starve them by taking away government
rations. And all these things happened. Countless Black
Mississippians were hanged, shot, and drowned for trying
to vote.

Roy Wilkins, the former executive director of the NAACP,
famously said in 1963, "There is no state with a record that
approaches that of Mississippi in inhumanity, murder, brutality, and racial hatred. . . . It is at the bottom of the list."
But maybe Nina Simone's famous protest song, "Mississippi
Goddamn," better explains the terror that was Mississippi.
And then there was the death of Emmett Till, the murder of
Medgar Evers, and the countless Black bodies at the bottom
of the river in the Mississippi Delta.

*　　*　　*

On the surface, the Freedom Project had three goals: bring
nearly a thousand northern young people (most of them
turned out to be white) to help register Black voters; start
freedom schools; and create the Mississippi Freedom Democratic Party as an alternative to the all-white Democratic

Party. But a recent *Politico* story described the Black architects of Freedom Summer, like Bob Moses, as having an astute but cold-blooded agenda:

> The new plan provoked sharp controversy, particularly
> among battle tested SNCC workers who rejected the im-
> plication that they needed white students to save the
> movement. But with backing from local Black activists,
> who were "very pragmatic," as one SNCC coordinator
> observed, Moses's plan carried the day. The architects
> of Freedom Summer were under no illusions. They never
> imagined that the young white summer volunteers
> would manage to register large numbers of voters, suc-
> ceeding where veteran civil rights workers had failed.
> Rather, they believed that the press "would respond to
> the beating of a Yale student as it simply would not do
> to the beating of a local Negro," as one SNCC leader later
> explained.

At the time, Moses said the white students brought with
them the power of their big schools and the influence of their
white parents. James Forman, the executive director of SNCC,
admitted years later that they were attempting to enlist "a
counter power elite."

* * *

Prior to arriving in Mississippi that summer, Dad and Uncle
Stokely had a near-death experience in Maryland when dozens of national guardsmen gassed them. Shortly after that,
they traveled to Oxford, Ohio, where they and other Black

SNCC workers trained the white Ivy Leaguers on what they were about to experience in Mississippi.

Bob Moses, the calm and charismatic Black math teacher from New York City, had managed to survive Mississippi, despite spending years traveling in the most dangerous parts of the Delta to encourage local Black Mississippians to register to vote. Both Moses and my dad would earn graduate degrees at Harvard after Freedom Summer. In 1982, Moses received the MacArthur Genius Grant, and that same year he created the Algebra Project, which helped children from low-income areas develop science and math skills.

Bob Moses was a family friend. He was one of the many "uncles" who were part of my village. I remember seeing him on panels with my dad, and I'd be in awe just watching these luminaries discuss what happened in the Delta that summer. A native of Harlem, Moses followed Ella Baker's suggestion to go to Mississippi in 1961, where he became the director of the Mississippi project. He traveled to Pike and Amite Counties, where he created a small network of locals to help him register voters. Even though Black people made up the majority in both counties, they had been closed out of the voting process since 1890.

Moses endured threats, assault, and the death of colleagues. Two activists, Herbert Lee and Louis Allen, who worked closely with him were murdered for trying to register Black people to vote.

In August 1961, Moses accompanied two Mississippians to the courthouse in Amite County in order to register to vote, but they were stopped by the sheriff's cousin, who brutally beat Moses with a blunt object. Several white people watched the attack but did nothing. Moses, however, did something no other Black person in the area had done: he filed assault and battery charges against his white attacker. During the trial, the judge told Moses to leave the courtroom before the jury returned the verdict because he couldn't protect him. Of course, the attacker was acquitted.

By 1964, Bob Moses had become not only one of the most important architects of Freedom Summer but also a folk hero to the white Freedom volunteers and a highly respected leader to Black SNCC workers. During the orientation in Ohio, he warned the white youngsters that they should expect death in Mississippi. Ella Baker, his mentor, had already warned the Black SNCCers that there should be no interracial dating in the Delta. Initially, the tension was thick between the SNCC workers and the white volunteers because the white students had no understanding that they were in a war zone without weapons, but all that would change.

* * *

It was during this orientation that Dad learned that Goodman, Chaney, and Schwerner were missing. Moses was speaking in front of the packed auditorium in Oxford, which was filled with volunteers and SNCC workers, when someone walked up to him and whispered in his ear that the three had not been heard from. Moses looked down and said, "They're dead." Although the bodies had not been found and there was no evidence yet that the trio had been killed, he knew for sure they were not alive and wanted to be straight with the volunteers. He wanted them to know that bad things were going to happen in Mississippi, and they had to decide if they were going to continue on to the state or not. "I'm going to Mississippi," he said.

To understand what happened to the three men, my father always says you need to understand what it was like to be a civil rights worker back then in Mississippi. While everyone knew the Freedom workers were coming, it was important that white racists in Mississippi didn't know who they were or what they were doing. One official bragged in the news about his town's preparation, which included 450 police officers, horses, dogs, 200 shotguns, tear gas and masks, searchlight trucks, and detention compounds.

Dad described the local Black people in Mississippi as the most beautiful people in the whole universe. They fed the Black and white volunteers with whatever they had, which was usually powdered eggs and government-issued cheese and chicken.

"They'd make liver pudding," Dad said. "Them white kids knew nothing about liver pudding." Their homes were modest— Dad remembers one family having dirt floors—but strangely the wealthy white volunteers loved being there, and some never returned home.

"These white kids were so happy they didn't know what to do," Dad said. "It was the first time they were treated like decent human beings. At home and school, they were told what to do and how to become this elite person. But in Mississippi, the Black people would do the best they could and put it out there: 'If you want some more food, just let me know because I got it here waiting for you.'"

It wasn't a culture shock for the white kids but a cultural change. Case in point: these Black Mississippi families didn't have inside bathrooms, so the white kids had to learn how to use the outhouse. The Black Mississippians would say, "There's the toilet paper. Bring it back when you come back." There was also a bucket with holes at the bottom that hung up on a pole. There would be a ladder next to the pole so you could pour water in the bucket, and that was your shower.

"Let me tell you about the breakfast," Dad always says, nearly bursting out laughing. "The meat on the table was from the pig tail to pig snoot. The white kids ain't never had that much pork in their life, but they sat there and enjoyed it." When a Jewish student would say, "Because of my religion, I don't eat pork," the families would go ahead and make that adjustment. "You were like one of their kids," Dad said.

They were good people, these Black Mississippians, but they were not into the nonviolent movement when people were killing them left and right. Dad recalls that when he was staying over at one family's home, the patriarch explained things to him just before bed. The father pointed to a window and a gun lying against it. "That's my window and gun." He pointed to other windows and said, "That's my wife's window and gun, and that's my son's window and gun. But since y'all nonviolent, you stay in the bedroom if anything happens."

Dad believes Freedom Summer was a turning point for the SNCCers. It was about that time they started veering away from the nonviolence movement after watching these Black Mississippians protect themselves from harm and terror.

* * *

On Sundays, the families would invite the workers to church, but not just any church. They knew that during the latter part of the summer, churches celebrated anniversaries and hosted events for renovation funds, and each event had a big dinner. Not only were the workers well-fed at these events but they could bring food home with them.

Although Dad also grew up in the rural South, the Delta residents saw the Black SNCCers as special, calling them "Martin Luther King's brothers and sisters." Dad recalled, "At dinner, they'd sit and smile the whole time we'd be sitting there." These Black Mississippians put their trust in the Freedom workers. "But you'd end up having to say, 'There is no way I'm going to be able to protect you. But I will go down to the courthouse with you to try to get you registered,'" Dad said.

Though most of the locals were not going to risk being seen at the courthouse with them, they supported the volunteers and workers however they could. The Black Mississippians who often hung around the courthouse acted meek around white folk. In reality, they were spies.

When Dad shook hands with the mayor of a local town, just to let him know he wasn't scared, the Black people who were hanging out at the courthouse that day spread the news. Before Dad could get back to headquarters, the incident was known among the locals.

The farmers had fresher food than others, and they filled the young people's bellies with a dinner of ham hocks, collard greens, buttermilk cornbread, candied yams, and black-eyed peas. The Black sharecroppers would tell the SNCC workers and the white volunteers to come by the house on a particular day. Dad and the rest of the volunteers would ask, "How many people can we bring?" They'd say, "You can bring 'round five."

Then they'd say, "Y'all go 'round back and pick some peas to feed the rest of 'em." Most of the Black people in the Delta worked as domestics or were unemployed, and some were sharecroppers; all were very different from the middle-class, educated SNCC workers like my father. Despite all their education, the Black and white civil rights workers needed to depend on the Black locals if they wanted to live another day. The great Ella Baker told my dad and the others that the way to do it was to blend in, dressing like the Black farmers and acting like the locals. "You have to see a picture of Stokely riding a mule," Dad often recalls, always with a hearty laugh.

Bob Moses, who grew up in the projects of New York City, was the best at blending in; he became famous for his overalls and horn-rimmed glasses. Many of the workers wore farmer bibs, which looked like aprons, and secretly stayed with Black sharecroppers. Sometimes they slept in the fields, and sometimes in the house. Dad told me the bibs came in handy because you could lay on them all day and then you could sleep in them all night.

* * *

Mass meetings in the churches became very important because that's where the workers distributed information, that's how they got people together, and that's how they got organized. "We had teams that would go out to various counties. We'd go out to see if we could find some people who were interested in civil rights and the right to vote, the right to control your own destiny, your life, the right to be free," Dad recalled. "And in doing so, we'd find two or three people. And then we said, 'Okay, well, now we have two or three people, let's go to the next level and let's see if we can find a place where we can assemble and talk about some of these things, so we can get more people together and let other locals know we are planning to be in the area and we want to organize.'"

While the Black ministers were wary of the volunteers, and especially the Black SNCC workers, the churches were meeting spaces where the locals would get updated on what the civil rights workers had done and would be doing. Those who listened were brave souls who often paid a price for their valor. The volunteers created tent cities for locals who were put out of their rented homes for being politically active. If a church was torched, the Freedom workers and volunteers surveyed the damage and began raising money to rebuild.

"That happened to one of our churches," Dad remembered. "We went over, and we looked at the church, and we started talking about how we are going to build it back. That simply meant that we had to set up some fundraising for them and get them out talking about the church in the community and talking about a fundraising campaign in order to show people that if they burn it down, we are going to build it back."

The church burnings were a tremendous loss because they were the most valuable properties that African Americans actually owned. The church burnings and deaths also caused a lot of mental and emotional anguish among the Freedom workers.

Dad said young people, some barely out of high school, had to ask themselves, *Did I cause this?* "That's a real adult kind of question. It made many of us grow up really quick."

* * *

In June 1964, Michael Schwerner, Andrew Goodman, and James Chaney were dealing with this dilemma. Schwerner, a young Jewish man from New York, had been training and working in Mississippi for two months. Goodman, another New Yorker, had just arrived. And Chaney, who was Black, was born and raised in the area and had been working with Schwerner.

"They received a call while in Ohio during the orientation," Dad explained. "The church they were using in Philadelphia, Mississippi, had burned down. That's why they drove back to Mississippi to see what they could find out and to let parishioners know what they discovered. They also wanted people to know they were going to put a plan together, so they could get that church rebuilt."

The police got wind of what the three men were doing. On June 21, the three were abducted by police officers and Klansmen and then shot. Their bodies were discovered two months later, finally shining the spotlight on brutal Mississippi. When they received news of the men's disappearance, Bob Moses, my father, and the other Black SNCC workers knew right away that the men were dead, though the naive white volunteers kept up hope. If they were in jail, the Black

SNCCers reasoned, the white terrorists wouldn't kill them because of the bad publicity. Moses, my father, and the other Black SNCC workers hadn't received a call from the three workers, which also alerted them that something was terribly wrong.

You see, the Freedom workers had built in a number of precautions. "There was a security code we had. If you were not going to return at the hour that you say you were going to return, you had to call," Dad said. "You had an hour and a half or two hours in which you had to call. If you didn't call in that time, then we started working with the FBI and the local police. We had CB radios in our cars, so you could call in and call around and somebody would be able to pick up on you, which allowed you to get messages through."

Dad also said they had a switch in the car that would turn the back lights off. If you were being followed at night, you could turn down a dirt road, flip the switch, and ease off the road to the right or to the left. The dust would also help to hide you, so you could get rid of the people tailing you.

"Everyone knew you didn't sit near a car window with a light behind you," Dad said, "because the silhouette would be red."

Goodman, Chaney, and Schwerner knew they were supposed to call the headquarters at a specific time, but they never did. Dad recalls that the searchers were divided in four different groups; his small group left Ohio, where the orientation was happening, at three in the morning and arrived in Mississippi several hours later. Unbeknownst to Dad, Stokely—who was in another small group—went missing too. He had been arrested but was later released.

When Dad describes the search he was involved in, it becomes clear how brave and skillful the poor Black share-croppers were. These simple farmers were all from around Philadelphia, Mississippi, where the three men went miss-ing. They hid Dad and the other civil rights workers in their homes; they fed them large meals of ham hocks and greens. They drove their pickup trucks in the dark night, speeding blindly and skillfully down terrains and hills and pointing out places where dead bodies could be buried. They kept clear of hound dogs and watchmen who used spotlights to find them; they knew what roads the Ku Klux Klan would be man-ning; and they hid Dad and the others in their homes during the day. Without these sharecroppers, Dad, Uncle Stokely, and the others wouldn't have survived a day. Dad returned to the headquarters in Meridian, Mississippi, once they got word the KKK knew they were searching for the three bodies, and now the KKK were searching for them.

* * *

Less than a year after Freedom Summer, civil rights work-ers continued to be terrorized by police. The story of Jimmie Lee Jackson is one I won't forget. Jimmie was a young, un-armed Black man who was beaten and shot in February 1965 by white state troopers in Alabama. His story is etched in my brain because my dad would always talk about Jimmie Lee Jackson in the context of the civil rights struggle. He was twenty-six when he was killed. We talk a lot about Emmett Till, but for many of the civil rights activists, Jimmie was the epitome of what it meant to be terrorized by white folk back then. As a woodcutter, Jimmie made $6 per week, but he got respect on Sundays, as he was the youngest deacon in his church.

Black people were eligible to vote in Alabama, but only 1 percent were registered at the time. Inspired by Martin Luther King, who had come to Alabama to speak, Jimmie—along with his mother and grandfather—had tried many times to register to vote in their hometown of Marion, Alabama. On February 18, he was one of five hundred people marching in Marion from a church to the local prison where a well-known activist had been jailed. As the protesters headed back to the church, police turned off the streetlights and began clubbing them as well as a few journalists (one photographer was beaten so badly he had to be hospitalized). Jimmie, his mother, his maternal grandfather, and his sixteen-year-old sister fled to a local café, where police followed them. When his mother tried to stop officers from beating Jimmie, one officer started beating her. Jimmie tried to guard his mother and grandfather, which is when another officer shot him twice in the stomach. Jimmie fled out of the café and was beaten more by the same officers. He died eight days later in the hospital. It is believed his death inspired the marches in Alabama, which led to Bloody Sunday, when six hundred civil rights marchers led by John Lewis, who was only twenty-five at the time, were brutally attacked by authorities as they crossed the Edmund Pettus Bridge in Selma.

* * *

The unfortunate truth about the murder of Medgar Evers in 1963, the murder of Jimmie Lee Jackson in 1965, the mass killings in Charleston in 2015, the police killing of Andrew

Brown Jr. in 2021, and the mass murders in Buffalo in 2022 is that they all prove there is a continuous line of Black folk dying at the hands of white terrorists, and this causes me real pain. No other race in this country has had to worry every single moment for decades about state-sanctioned violence and domestic racial terrorism.

6

WHITE TERROR, PART 2

Legal Genocide

The common bond between my father's political and emotional struggles and the present-day obstacles we face is the shedding of Black blood. The pain that's associated with the Black experience in this country is generational. There's a common line that can be drawn from the Emmett Tills and the Jimmie Lee Jacksons all the way to the Walter Scotts and the Andrew Browns. The only difference these days, as Ella Baker once said, is that the murderers traded their white robes for black robes.

A big element of white terror that we don't often talk about is how the law justifies the killing of Black men and women. As a civil rights lawyer who goes into courtrooms all across the country, I see how they're killing us in the courtroom as well as in the street.

Ben Crump, the civil rights lawyer who represented George Floyd, calls it "legalized genocide." He once said to me:

They kill our children on the streets and then in the courts; they killed Trayvon again with "stand your ground." They killed Breonna Taylor again with this intellectual justification of discrimination. It's legalized genocide of colored people. That's the fear and the pain, the suffering and anxiety that Black people have every day of their lives. We wake up in the morning and our children go out of the house, [and] we pray that it doesn't happen to my child because you know, if it does, oftentimes the law would justify it.

*　　*　　*

The rushing wind can be heard on the body cam video as a SWAT truck packed with seven sheriff's deputies swept down a Black neighborhood in Elizabeth City, North Carolina, and converged onto Andrew Brown's residence. I still shake my head when I think it took a whole task force to deliver a couple of drug-related warrants at 8:45 in the morning. When the deputies pulled up, forty-two-year-old Andrew, who was in his car talking on his cell phone, backed away into a vacant lot, which is when three of the seven deputies shot him multiple times, including in the back of the head. The medical examiner deemed his death a homicide. Andrew had no weapons, and the whole incident was caught on body cam. Nevertheless, the district attorney would call the killing justified and treated us, the family's Black attorneys, like we were the enemies.

Andrew Brown's legal case is just one example of white terror in modern-day America. From the grave, Andrew has shown the world how a legal system has evolved and perpetrated the death of yet another Black man. His case, as frustrating as it still is to me, allowed America to get a real glimpse into our flawed, racist legal process, a process that must be dismantled if we are truly going to evolve into the world I want my children to live in.

As Harry Daniels, one of the lead attorneys on Andrew Brown's case, said:

> White terror used to be when white people could burst into an old Black sharecropper's shack to grab a twelve-year-old grandson who might have whistled at a white woman and kill him by drowning him and wrapping a motor around his neck. These days it's the police killing unarmed Black men and getting away legally with it. That's the new white terror.

*   *   *

Andrew Brown's case took on a life of its own because it was the first nationally publicized police murder after George Floyd's death. People thought policing had changed, which is weird to me. Andrew himself was an imperfect messenger, not unlike George Floyd. He had a criminal record. He lived "the life," but anyone who knew Andrew would say that he tried to take care of his kids and he never carried weapons, which is an important part of his narrative and the story of white terror in America right now. His family called me from the mortuary. Harry Daniels, a civil rights lawyer based in downtown Atlanta, had been called by the family on the day of the shooting. A former air force veteran who fought in the war in Iraq, Harry is also a former law enforcement officer.

Early that evening, his wife met him at the airport in Atlanta with two suits in a garment bag. "I'm a bulldog," Harry says. "I'm tough like my mama. Don't think you're going to piss in our face and tell us it's raining."

Several days after Andrew's death, Harry picked up Ben Crump from the airport. We met that night over a fish dinner someone brought us. There are only two hotels in Elizabeth City, the Fairfield Inn and the Hampton Inn. I stayed at the Fairfield Inn with Ben Crump for a couple of nights. Harry was at the Hampton Inn.

Ben and I meet each other in the most random places. Not long ago, I was speaking at the Botham Jean Foundation, where I ran into Ben once again. Botham was a twenty-six-year-old man who was killed by an off-duty Dallas police officer who claimed she entered his apartment by mistake, thinking it was hers. That day, Ben brought Philonise Floyd, the brother of George Floyd, to support the Jean family. By the time of Andrew Brown's death, Ben had already become one of my best friends. He's somebody I look up to. He's a plain, simple man. When we get to a city, he goes shopping at Walmart and Target to get his clothes and suits. He eats a hamburger well-done, with ketchup and mustard. If you go to a nice restaurant, he gets fried shrimp and fries. And every Sunday, he's in church with his family. He is a legend, truly, but he's a legend because of the work that he puts in. And he's a legend because of the fact that he's very good at what he does.

Only in his early fifties, he has been compared to the icons and luminaries of the legal profession, particularly Black lawyers, although he's started his own path. In this new social media era, there are always people who have some criticism of

Ben. But none of it really sticks because people don't know or understand the work he does, the services he provides to the families he represents, how he's there through thick and thin, and how every case he takes isn't a million-dollar case. In fact, the Terence Crutcher and Botham Jean families haven't seen $1 yet, but he's still working and working and working diligently, not just to get them some success in the court of law but also to change laws so that other families don't have to go through what they do.

When Ben speaks, you hear his plain language, and you hear Tallahassee, Florida, where he practices; you hear Lumberton, North Carolina, where he grew up. What you are really hearing is the South. But what one cannot discount is that there's no one who knows civil rights law better than Ben, and this area of the law is probably one of the most important when it comes to Black folk.

* * *

The threats Ben and I see now are not unlike the threats Uncle Stokely and Dad experienced back in the 1960s. The only difference is that the threats today often come through social media. I usually don't pay attention to being called a "nigger" on Twitter, but in early 2022 I knew something was wrong as I went through my messages on Instagram. I noticed a series of messages from one account: "U Niggers full of shit, like Yankee whitey" and "We will defend ourselves from commie porn politicians" and "Shit gonna hit the fan." Some of the texts included YouTube videos of me on CNN; some were direct threats, and most didn't make sense. This digital stalker was speaking in non sequiturs, and the messages came in flurries, fast and furious when I was on CNN, and intermittently when I wasn't. I think he'd send them after watching me on TV.

The messages and threats arrived between February 25 and March 24, but I didn't see all of them until March. I reached out to Pete Strom, my boss and owner of the law firm that employs me, and sent him the messages. He told me to report them. The escalation of the threats, the stalker's claim that he had guns and appreciated the Confederacy, and his belief that Black boys were bringing down his community with drugs and were killing white girls—all of that rang the alarm. I didn't know who he was, but I soon discovered his name was Grant Edward Olson Jr. He was forty-eight and worked at a motel in Asheville, North Carolina. He was apparently a good employee but had racist views and did indeed own guns.

The thing about social media is that you don't see the person behind the message. If he had said some of those things to me, I would have punched him in his face, but my biggest fear was for my family. In a press release, I wrote, "This isn't just about me. I have a wife, a teenager bonus daughter, and twin three-year-olds, and I take any threats against them very seriously." In April, Olson was arrested and accused of intimidating me for exercising my civil rights as an attorney, lobbyist, and commentator.

Not unlike me, Ben Crump receives hundreds, if not thousands, of threats. Whereas I learned to protect myself by looking at how my father endured all that hate and terror back in the '60s, Ben has followed in the path of former Supreme Court justice Thurgood Marshall.

"I don't take the death threats lightly," Ben said. "But I am a disciple of Thurgood Marshall. Every time he went to a city, all the Black people were happy, but also, the other side of the coin was that the white people and all the white supremacists and all the KKK also knew he was coming too, and they were all plotting against him. Very frequently, he would have to move from house to house every night because the lynch mob was trying to get him."

Similarly, Ben is rarely anywhere more than a day or two. "You just have to take into consideration your family," he told me. "You want to be able to make sure that the sick people out there do not do something that will break your family's heart forever."

Every time Ben gets one of these crazy phone calls or racist emails or social media threats, he contacts the FBI. "But Bakari," he said, "even with all that we do to protect ourselves, I'll say this, I won't let them intimidate us or have fear, and I believe there are some things worth dying for. Not only do the enemies of equality got to know that, but more importantly, our children got to know that we believe in their future so much that we're willing to sacrifice it all."

Maybe so, but we are not willing to sacrifice our family. For Ben, white terror has been a lifelong conversation he's had with his own children, two grown men in their twenties and one daughter who's eight. He even developed sayings and poems to make them remember that you are a target. He tells them to never let your guard down. While you're shopping, banking, or especially having anything to do with the court, you are a target, he warns.

"I have to always remind my boys because my youngest, Chancellor, he's an activist, and oftentimes, they engage with authority very defiantly," Ben told me. "I say that you can be right, but they won't perceive that as right. They will perceive you are wrong, and that can cost you your life. We tell him to call us; you don't try to deal with it yourself. You don't try to tell them you know the law."

Ben tells his activist son exactly what my father has always told me: "Don't try to tell them that they don't have no right. Don't ask what's their probable cause. The time to challenge the police is not on the side of the road; the time to challenge the police is in a court of law with your parents and good lawyers."

. . .

Back in North Carolina, we were all part of Andrew Brown's funeral procession, though I usually don't do funerals. I have a fear of death; I've had it since I was a child. My mother believes it stems from all those days I sat at my father's knee, listening to him discuss all the deaths he'd seen in the 1960s and the day he was shot during the Orangeburg massacre. As a little boy, I knew the families of James Chaney, Andrew Goodman, and Michael Schwerner, and I was free to ask them questions. Maybe that's the cause of the anxiety I developed during childhood, which I still have to this day. At least, that is what my mother believes. It always bothered her to see me crying in a pew, watching my tearful father tell the story of the massacre and the terror of Freedom Summer.

. . .

The three of us—Ben, Harry, and I—all spoke at Andrew's passing ceremony, along with Al Sharpton and the Reverend

William Barber. "Here we are again," I said to the crowd of mourners that day. "To many, it's just another Black body."

There was a horse-drawn carriage by the water. People were out on the streets watching the demonstrators and the police, who were everywhere. The crowds and protesters remained for one hundred days. Andrew Brown's death was the number one story in the world for about a week. Every time we did a press conference, all the major news stations carried it live. *Good Morning America* carried us. We did *Dateline*, we did NBC—there wasn't a news channel we didn't do.

What really brought us attorneys together is that we had all heard from family and eyewitnesses that Andrew Brown had been shot in the back of the head, which means he was trying to get away from the deputies. We couldn't prove this without seeing the footage. The district attorney was saying Andrew tried to kill the officers with his car. Meanwhile, a group of media organizations had filed a lawsuit to get the videos, which led us to the sheriff's office, where we were told the family would get to see the body cam recordings.

The scene that day in Elizabeth City was like something out of a movie. "Did you see the movie *Time to Kill*?" Harry later said. "Well, this was just like *Time to Kill*."

People were everywhere: media from across the globe, protesters, the Black Panthers. Drones were flying around, helicopters soared above us, and snipers stood on the roof of the sheriff's building.

Despite the activity, it was calm outside compared to the fire happening inside the sheriff's office. The county attorney had delayed the meeting while the faces of the officers in the video were being blurred. When our legal team entered the sheriff's administrative office, we found forty deputies in army fatigues lining the wall.

The dispute between us lawyers and the county attorney began when he refused to allow us to see the body cam video. He incorrectly interpreted case law and decided that only the family could see the video, and then only a North Carolina lawyer.

Outside, people waited in the heat, and the media kept their eyes on the door of the sheriff's office. "Everyone is sort of on bated breath here, waiting to see what the attorneys will say, if they will describe any of the video that they have seen inside," a CNN reporter said. "And of course, the video itself was a few minutes' long, we would think. So the fact that they spent about more than an hour in there, perhaps there were many discussions in there. We're waiting to see what the attorneys can share with us about that meeting."

* * *

We all gathered inside a back room in the sheriff's office. Besides us lawyers, there was also a Black lieutenant, the county attorney, and the sheriff. When the county attorney incorrectly interpreted the law, Harry showed him the case law, but still he refused to allow us to see the video.

"No, no, no, we are not going to do this," Mike Cox, the Pasquotank County Attorney, said as he started to walk off. "I agreed to the family seeing some of the videos, but not you."

Harry was livid. "Mike, what's going on here?" he said. "We represent the families. We can see it."

Cox refused, getting angrier and redder by the moment.

"What the hell! Are you kidding me?" Harry said. Harry

later told us, "Of course he doesn't want us to see the video because he knows we can describe it in detail to the media."

Eventually, Ben told Harry to let me talk to Cox, explaining that I was the most diplomatic of the three of us. "Let's let Bakari smooth it over."

Harry smiled and said, "Go right ahead, but he's not going to let Bakari see that video."

All three of us knew we were fighting a losing battle because the county attorney held the video, not us. And the district attorney was still claiming that Andrew tried to hit the officers and that the car he was driving made contact. Worse, the district attorney and Cox shared an office with the sheriff's deputies and knew all the deputies involved.

I think most people who are acquainted with me know that my demeanor is really mild. I'm not an argumentative person. I can talk. I can slice through conversations, but I am not confrontational. That day, however, my patience was tried.

The state statute that Mike Cox cited clearly says an attorney representing the family is allowed to see the body cam footage. But Cox insisted, "No, you have to be licensed in North Carolina."

I replied, "I think you're wrong. Let's call the attorney general to get an opinion really quick because, as a county attorney, you're making a really bad decision. I don't think you're making this decision prudently."

His response was argumentative: "I will not be fucking bullied by you or anybody else."

I was hot! I asked him, "Who do you think you're talking to?" He stormed out, and I followed. The sheriff apologized, and the lieutenant just shook his head. I told everybody we were leaving. I had never been in a situation with that lack of professionalism. As a personal matter, I had never had anyone talk to me like that who was that . . . little in stature, and that bothered me.

Outside the office building, I told the world what happened. Later that day, we met with Andrew Brown's son, Andrew's aunt, and Chantel Cherry-Lassiter, who was Andrew's family attorney and friend, to explain what was happening with Cox. We then sent Chantel in to review the video since she was the only licensed attorney from North Carolina on our team. Along with one of Andrew's adult sons, they saw twenty seconds of a highly redacted body cam video, but she believed she had the answer.

Several weeks later, a judge ruled that family members could see the heavily redacted body cam videos. Meanwhile, the county attorney and district attorney, who are supposed to be on the side of justice and helping the families of murder victims fight for it, continued to insist that the shooting was lawful and that Andrew was using his vehicle to hurt the deputies.

Chantel told the world that Andrew never tried to hit the officers, but the deputies actually ran up to the car, touching it as Andrew was trying to drive away. The only way our legal team could prove that the shooting was unjustified was to see more of the video. The district attorney had viciously and publicly attacked Chantel, calling her a liar and threatening to disbar her, which meant we couldn't use the only North Carolina lawyer on our team.

Harry took Chantel aside and promised her we'd avenge

her name, but we needed help. He later told us, "I have the right person. He's a former law school classmate." And Harry trusted him. Chance Lynch was a former district attorney as well as a pastor; he was not only articulate and used to speaking in public but was also in good standing within the state.

"He has the pedigree we need," Harry assured us.

Chance is about my age and two years younger than Harry. Like me, he has two very young children. Whereas Harry is a self-described bulldog, Chance is something altogether different. A short, stodgy, light-skinned brother, Chance is an old soul trapped in a hip-hop body. He's been an ordained minister since he was a teen, but he also collects Jordans. He is a weird convergence of a lot of different things, which makes him a good lawyer. He has the skills needed to pay attention to detail and take copious notes. He's from Pitt County in North Carolina, where his family is well-known and loved.

Like everyone else in America, Chance had been watching us on television, but I am not sure he knew what we were against. On the morning Harry called, Chance was working from home, finishing his morning routine with his two daughters, feeding them chocolate muffins and milk. Harry asked whether he could get to the superior courthouse in Elizabeth City in two hours. There was a hearing at noon to decide if the video of Andrew's death could be shared with the family. Without hesitation, Chance said he was happy to help.

The entire courthouse was basically shut down for our hearing. The legal team met on the second floor of the courthouse, while Chance was escorted past the press pool and a large crowd of onlookers outside to meet us. I didn't know Chance at the time, but he would become an important part of our legal team. After the hearing, we decided he'd be the North Carolina attorney who would get to see the video of Andrew's last moments in two weeks' time. I can imagine it was an enormous amount of pressure for Chance to suddenly be thrown in this situation; he'd have to sit by Andrew Brown's two sons and watch their father be shot over and over. He would see more than Chantel got to see, but we were not sure what was in the rest of the footage.

When fighting for justice, a lawyer has to be many things, including a psychologist, all at the same time. You must be compassionate and say to the grieving family, "If you need a minute, let's stop and help manage your anger." You can imagine the anger that Andrew's family would be feeling while in that room.

When we got to the courthouse on the day of the viewing, we could barely get out of the car. We could barely walk because the crowd was so big. Here's what Chance had to say about that moment: "The crowd just thought I was a guy walking with the legal team. They didn't know that I was the one actually going in. Everybody was asking Bakari questions or asking Harry questions, and I was standing right there but no one said anything to me, because who am I?"

He walked in with Andrew's two sons and was greeted by the sheriff and some of his deputies, who shook his hand. Of course, they all knew who he was. "I didn't even have to introduce myself," Chance recalled. "They said, 'You can follow us; we will show you where to go.'"

Riding the elevator upstairs didn't take long, probably not a minute, but to Chance it felt like an eternity. He told Andrew's sons, "You know what we're about to see? If you need a moment, just let me know. We'll stop. If you need time, take your time. We'll get through it together. I'm right here with you. Don't feel like you're in this by yourself." They said they understood and thanked him, saying, "I'm so glad you're with us."

Chance and Andrew's sons entered the room and sat down in front of a big flat-screen TV. There were two other men in the room, a Black officer standing over by the door and a white guy operating the television and the video for them. "Both of them were very nice," Chance recalled. "I sat down at a table with my notebooks and my pens. Andrew's sons sat to my left. We sat right in front of the television so that we could see everything."

Chance later said that he was more nervous going in because he didn't know what he was going to see. The last thing he wanted was to have to say, "Yes, Andrew tried to run them all over." He remembered thinking, *God, please don't let this be a video where I got to come out and say that because I'm going to be honest. I'm not going to lie.*

When Chance and Andrew's sons sat down in the viewing room, the man operating the computer clicked on a file, and the video popped up on the big television screen in front of them. "Stop, go back, play that again, stop, go back, ten more seconds," Chance would later tell him.

How hard it must have been for Andrew's sons to have to watch their father's death on a big screen over and over in order to prove his death was unjustified, but that's what many Black families are having to do. That's what Andrew's sons had to do, and they did it for two or three hours.

The first video was from a dashcam, which made it hard to

see or hear anything, but the second video, from a body camera, showed a lot more. Chance and Andrew's sons could see the deputies on the back of the SWAT team's pickup truck, but what they were saying had been redacted. The truck passed blocks of houses, but it was hard to know where the truck was going until it turned and came to an abrupt stop. From that moment, they heard doors slamming and people jumping off the truck. They heard a bunch of cussing, yelling, and "Put your effing hands up! Let me see your hands!" Andrew's sons could see their father sitting in his car, completely startled. He looked like he was on his phone.

"There was more yelling and 'Put your hands up!' Andrew backed up, putting his distance between them," Chance recalled. "Andrew turned his steering wheel to a hard left. When he does, there's a gunshot. . . . Then he drives between them and on the video, you can see where they run to the pavement that's in his yard, like a driveway. They run to the edge of that while he's well across the yard. There is just fire—*bah, bah, bah, bah, bah, bah, bah, bah, bah, bah*."

Chance said that while the deputies are shooting, you could see the kill shot, and you could see the tracks where the car veers off the road. It was as if Andrew was driving straight, but then when they shot him, the car veers and goes down the ditch and into the tree across the street.

"They fired multiple shots," Chance said. "We were able to count thirteen." When they got to the car in the video, the deputies still had their guns drawn and commanded Andrew to get out of the car or put his hands up.

"But he's dead," Chance explained. "They open the door. You see his body is taken out. They actually lay him down on the ground with his face in the ground, and you can see the bullet hole in the back of his head."

Chance said that's when Andrew Brown's two sons grew more distressed. "I remember them yelling and cussing and just very upset. I don't remember them crying, but I just remember them being very expressive. I gave them a minute to calm down. . . . They grew more upset when the deputies were shooting because it was just ridiculous. This man is driving nowhere near them, going away from them, and they just unloaded." One of the sons said to the officers in the room, "Have y'all seen this? You can't tell me this is right."

While they were watching the videos, Chance and the sons could hear the people outside chanting Andrew Brown's name. Meanwhile, Chance was able to go through the video as many times as needed.

"We were there long enough, the officers offered us something to drink. We declined. We thanked them, but no, we were good. When we were done, I asked his sons, 'Are y'all good? Did you want to see it again?' And they said no. I said, 'Sheriff, thank you, I'm good.'" Chance gathered his notebooks and pens and put it all in his briefcase, and the three of them walked out of the room and went down the elevator.

As Chance and Andrew Brown's sons rode down in the elevator, Chance knew this was a very important moment in all their lives. "I told them they were strong. They did a good job. I told them that I was honored to be able to help them with this. In my mind, I was thinking that I had to let my team know what I saw. . . . Andrew's family was downstairs waiting. . . . They depended on me because I'm the lawyer. I went in without anybody recognizing my role, but I came out that day feeling like the world waited to hear me speak about what I saw."

Chance confirmed what Chantel said, and to this day, no one publicly disputes it, but the fight is hardly over.

The Prescription

To help ensure that Black folk won't die at the hands of law enforcement, we need legislative action. In a perfect world, you would have Republican Tim Scott and Democrat Cory Booker introduce legislation that creates a nationwide database of law enforcement officers who commit bad acts. A database could prevent someone who got fired for brutalizing a person in Richmond, Virginia, from going to Washington, DC, and joining the force there. If they brutalized someone while at the Oakland, California, police department, they couldn't move to Los Angeles and become a part of the sheriff's department. There's a database for elder abuse and child abuse; we need a database for police abuse.

We could shield that database from the public, although I believe in transparency, and only let it be accessed by law enforcement agencies. This seems like the simplest idea, doesn't it?

There are other things we could do, such as ban choke holds and no-knock warrants—or at least agree to a prohibition against serving no-knock warrants after dark. Imagine if a stranger, particularly in the South (where everyone has the right to bear arms and does), attempts to burst in your house at 4 a.m. That's a bad situation, even for law enforcement, because you will shoot the intruder. No-knock warrants create tragic incidents like the one in which Latoya James was shot by police during a drug raid in Georgia, or Breonna Taylor was killed after seven police officers burst into her apartment. As a result of no-knock warrants, law enforcement officers sometimes kill individuals who were not named in the warrant.

In many cases of police abuse, the officer is not punished because of laws protecting them, but we could limit those laws. Qualified immunity protects law enforcement officers from liability arising from acts committed on duty, which is why so many officers who have killed unarmed Black people are not in prison. Limiting qualified immunity is a bit sticky as most people don't want police to have any skin in the game because of the inherent dangers of working in law enforcement.

I think that's absurd. In my opinion, an officer should have to put down $25,000 or $50,000 of their own money, maybe from their pension, when they commit an unlawful act. Right now, the state pays all settlement costs. An officer can kill someone, and the victim's family essentially pays for the settlement because in most instances taxpayers are responsible for that; law enforcement pays nothing. You'd be surprised how many officers have settled cases and are still on the force.

And so yes, there are policy prescriptions that would prevent the police killings we are seeing in the streets, that would prevent what happened to Andrew Brown and Eric Garner from happening again, but without fortitude from both sides of Congress, none of this will ever change.

7

DARK MONEY AND RACIST CAPITALISTS

Like the killings in Charleston, South Carolina, a few years earlier, the mass shooting at a Buffalo, New York, supermarket in 2022 took the best from us: those church ladies who wear the big hats and will pop you when you do wrong in church but also give you wise words when you need to hear them. They sit in the front two rows like queens, but they must decide whether to pay their utility bills or get groceries. The Buffalo shooting victims were the backbone of their community, taken from us for no other reason but because they were Black. They include seventy-seven-year-old Pearl Young, a substitute teacher who also taught Sunday school and ran a soup kitchen; eighty-six-year-old Ruth Whitfield, who had just been visiting her husband at a nursing home when she decided to go to the grocery store; and seventy-two-year-old Katherine Massey, a local activist.

What happened on May 14, 2022, at Tops Friendly Markets calls to mind yet another young white man, Dylann Roof, who drove miles and miles intent on killing Black people. Eighteen-year-old Payton Gendron, the hate-filled Buffalo shooter, drove two hundred miles from his hometown in Conklin, New York, to murder African Americans at the grocery store.

Dylann Roof chose Mother Emmanuel because it was a historical Black church in downtown Charleston. Payton also scouted out his killing field, choosing the only grocery store in a Black community on the east side of Buffalo. Wearing a tactical helmet and plated armor and armed to the teeth with a Bushmaster XM-15 rifle, he opened fire on fourteen people, killing ten of them, all of them Black. The grocery store he chose was the only one in that east Buffalo neighborhood because the area was "a food desert," a place where residents had no real access to low-cost groceries, but Payton didn't care about this.

Prior to the rampage, which Payton live streamed, he had foretold the horror in a 180-page manifesto. On his rifle, he wrote "Reparation this," and he went on Discord, an instant messaging platform, to talk about his discontent with society and about how Jews were conspiring to replace white people with Black and Brown folk. He had "researched" this shit because he got bored during COVID. Payton apologized for the killings during his sentencing, but he also admitted that his motives were racist and blamed online content for his bloody massacre.

Guess who entertained and educated extremists like Payton? Fox's former anchor Tucker Carlson poisoned the minds of countless viewers who believed, like Payton, that there was a plot to get rid of white people and to have mainly Black and

Brown people in power. And that's the crazy thing about poison like this; it may not kill you immediately, but eventually it will get you.

Tucker Carlson and other members of the dark money class, which supports think tanks that hide their hateful anti-Black and anti-Brown immigrant philosophies, are a cancer. Tucker and his ilk are also a poison. And what might be most disingenuous about him is that there's a possibility he really doesn't believe any of what he says. Look no further than the thousands of messages Fox was forced to release as part of the Dominion Voting Systems lawsuit against the network. In text messages, Carlson and his colleagues expressed serious doubts about Donald Trump's claims of voter fraud, but that's not what they said publicly.

What I am saying is that Tucker is likely playing us. One thing is clear: Tucker is a modern-day white terrorist in a bow tie. He is no less dangerous than the KKK members who, during Freedom Summer, tried to hunt down my father and the rest of the civil rights workers searching for the bodies of Chaney, Goodman, and Schwerner.

* * *

In 2016, I was traveling constantly to give political speeches and participate in debates all over the country and around the world. In a small airport, I can't remember which one, I bumped into Tucker Carlson. Tucker always seemed kind of dweebish to me. He was the epitome of what you would expect a prep boy to look like—with his penny loafers and khakis—but he never appeared to be dangerous or threatening. I stand over six feet four, and so to me Tucker isn't a big guy by any stretch, but he always had the look of a big rising star, smart enough to carry on conversations on the various television shows he hosted, from CNN's *Crossfire* to his stint on MSNBC.

Still, Tucker is a shell of what many people would say they knew him to be back then, although I would argue that the toxicity we are now seeing from him was probably always there. At first, he never seemed dangerous like the MAGAs or the extreme Republicans who come with the same ilk as Donald Trump. The transformation of the Republican Party and the rise of overtly racist displays of hate can be understood by studying Tucker's own transformation.

Just as Donald Trump achieved both financial and political status by using racism as political currency, media personalities like Tucker found success, both financially and in the ratings, by trafficking in the same garbage. Tucker's viewers—overwhelmingly older white men—treated the host's proclamations as the gospel while others used them to reinforce their preconceived notions and stereotypes. Tucker's show damaged everyone who consumed his poison, because the more you consume poison, the more likely you are to get sick from it.

Now there's a profit motive attached to someone like Trump or Tucker; there's a power motive to be gained too, because racism is the oldest wedge issue that we have in this country. The more you're able to divide individuals, the more you're able to get people to believe in the tropes of hypersexuality, toxicity, or hypermasculinity that they put on Black folk, or to believe that we are just predisposed to crime or that we can't make good decisions. And while all of those lies erode the fabric of democracy, people like Tucker get the fat-ass checks.

It's funny because they utilize the same tropes and reinforce them daily, and then they go out and get Herschel Walker to run for the US Senate, because as much as they use racism, it's not the ultimate goal. The goal is always power and money, especially dark money, for these individuals, and they just use racism to get there.

*   *   *

Tucker Carlson was born in San Francisco and raised mainly by his father, Dick Carlson, who was a reporter and television journalist. Dick eventually turned his back on journalism and accepted a variety of Republican appointments. Tucker's father was born to a fifteen-year-old mother who put him in an orphanage; Dick's father was so distraught that she wouldn't help him steal the baby out of the orphanage and marry him that he killed himself, according to a *Washington Post* article that Dick wrote in 1993. Tucker's mother came from a very wealthy California family. Unlike Tucker's father, she was an artist and "a bohemian," who Tucker claims abandoned him and his brother, Buckley, when Tucker was six. Dick eventually married another heiress, this one a child of privilege who came from the Swanson food empire, and who Tucker has called his "real mother."

As a young man, Tucker lived an affluent life of boarding schools. When his father eventually ran for office, Tucker, who started wearing a bow tie in middle school, was right beside him.

In 2011, Tucker received a call from a relative, explaining

that his biological mother was dying somewhere in France. It appeared she intended to disinherit her two sons, leaving them $1 in her will while everything else went to her current husband, including mineral rights to property she owned. However, according to court documents, the handwritten note was discovered after Tucker and his brother had already received funds from their mother's property, which eventually meant they could keep what they had already received. Tucker told his friend and former Fox anchor Megyn Kelly in 2017 that his mother abandoned them because she didn't like them. "If your mother doesn't like you," he said, "well, yeah . . . boo hoo. . . . It sounds terrible, but it's not up to you on how she feels. You really can't control how other people feel about you."

His relative suggested that he should go immediately to see his dying mother. He called Buckley, who said, "What? No, my son has a soccer game."

"I was like, 'Right. That's how I feel,'" Tucker said, further explaining he went out to eat dinner that night, feeling no guilt because he had already made peace long ago.

Whether his feelings about his free-spirited, left-wing mother contributed to his right-wing political views is something I will not speculate on, but here's something interesting. He said he's not bothered by criticism from people he doesn't like or care about, which he suggests is linked to his mother's dislike and abandonment of him. "I lived through that as a child. I'm not going through that again."

Tucker and I have never been friends, so I don't know if this is where his contempt for the left and progressive politics comes from, but I do believe he has other motivations. When we've met, he never appeared to be someone who was just a flat-out, stone-cold racist. The truth is I don't think Tucker believes all of his misstatements, overhyped facts, conspiracies, or warnings about illegal immigrants being used to build a base of power for the Democrats. (In fact, Hispanics in red states like Texas and Florida are increasingly voting Republican.)

The *New York Times* studied his every word on *Tucker Carlson Tonight* and found that his "escalating rhetoric and provocation on the air" was part of an effort to rebuild Fox's declining audience; he was very successful at it, drawing more television watchers than any other cable show. Before he was fired in 2023, Tucker was well aware that Newsmax and One America News Network, which are essentially fact-free zones offering platforms to fringe players in the conservative echo chamber, were drawing viewers away from Fox News.

While I'm not letting Tucker off the hook, because it is clear that he continues to use racism to gain wealth and influence, I do believe—and listen to me carefully—that if there was something else that was as divisive and as valuable as racism is, Tucker would use it. That doesn't absolve him. I think it probably makes him worse than the person who puts a cross in front of your yard.

In fact, it takes someone who lacks any type of fortitude to push these values and this ignorance to the people who probably are racist. I believe strongly we have to move away from always calling individuals who share different opinions about people of color, especially Black people, racist. I think that is insignificant because it doesn't do anything but raise the level of sensationalism. We have to understand why structures are what they are. If Tucker Carlson can be defined as a racist, so what? The real problem with Tucker is that he perpetuates a system of bigotry for personal gain. This is the greatest danger of someone like Tucker. Someone calling me "nigger" in a bathroom isn't nearly as big a deal as portraying racist stereotypes and tropes on TV for 3 million people to see, which he did twenty times a month. When folk come to me talking about Tucker, believing that he is telling the truth, I say there's nothing about the over-the-top xenophobia he displays that is an accurate depiction of our history, and Tucker knows this. But he has chosen to speak to those white people who believe they are under attack and no longer in the majority. It's a weird type of conversation or miseducation because it stems from the belief that white people built this country, that they didn't steal the land, and that they're entitled to everything.

Stoking the flames of hate on his Fox show has made Tucker more famous than he ever was on CNN, which might be when he turned to the dark side.

In 2004, Jon Stewart, the beloved *Daily Show* host, made a memorable appearance on CNN's *Crossfire*, which Tucker cohosted, and proceeded to take him down in the most epic way. Jon called Tucker a hack, said he was divisive, and famously concluded, "You're a dick."

*   *   *

Inspired by an exhaustive study by the *New York Times*, an anchor with National Public Radio hosted a show entitled "Has Tucker Carlson Created the Most Racist Show in the History of Cable News?" The *New York Times* reporter who investigated Tucker and his show said the Fox anchor helped shape the MAGA movement and declared him to be the most dangerous man on television. His research found that Tucker had borrowed language from neo-Nazis, nativists, and white nationalists who congregate on the infamous dark web to share theories and conspiracies.

The same reporter claimed in another interview that Tucker's weaponization of his viewers' fears and grievances was why he had the most watched cable show in the nation. "Every night," the reporter said, "he teaches fear and loathing."

. . .

The truth? Tucker is nothing special, and what he said on Fox was nothing new. I'm old enough to remember a time when being racist wasn't cool, but there were more periods in this country when political hucksters ruled the day: George Wallace, Richard Nixon, Ronald Reagan—these men were also peddling fears and racist theories. So, I continue to say Tucker is really nothing new—he's just as hateful as Bull Connor was in the 1950s and '60s.

Tucker is the clear definition of a racial capitalist. The entire American labor movement was deliberately tainted by industrial racism. Capitalists kept their employees disorganized, and white supremacy was used as a tool to divide workers by encouraging white workers to feel they were superior to Black workers and other immigrants. This was encouraged not so much because the power brokers hated Black people, though they might have (I'm from the South, so I understand that racist sentiments are real), but what I'm saying is the motivation to encourage superiority among poor whites was only so that the powers that be could capitalize off the hate. And this is exactly what Tucker is doing.

*　*　*

One night in early spring 2021, Tucker went on a rant on his show in which he gave an impassioned defense of the white supremacists' "great replacement" theory. It's a conspiratorial notion embraced mostly by those who are in the darkest corners of the internet, but Tucker cited it four hundred times on his show, shifting this fringe racist myth into the mainstream.

I am most aware of this when I am talking to white people I meet while playing golf or at work, especially in the South; most of them watch Fox News, unapologetically. That means they're consuming this racist bullshit espoused by Tucker, and you can see how far the country has fallen.

The theory that Tucker liked to talk about claims that conspirators are trying to replace the current electorate with more obedient voters from developing countries. He said that Black and Brown people are diluting the political power that used to belong to him and others like him. He couched this as a voting rights issue when it's really a matter of racism.

Payton Gendron, the young man who killed ten Black people in Buffalo, believed in the "great replacement" theory. When this was discovered, it sparked advertising boycotts of Tucker's show and calls for his firing, but nothing happened.

The Buffalo tragedy did not spark Fox to take him off the air. People were still watching him five nights a week as he played on their fear of losing power as the white population shrinks. After it was clear that Tucker wasn't going anywhere—even after it was made public that a mass murderer fell for the theory Tucker had been hyping—well-meaning people asked, "Why can't he be fired?" The answer was because he was bringing in huge sums of money for the network. Just think about the advertising revenue that his show pulled in. That's why he was not fired. These days, the white supremacists and their sympathizers have traded their hoods for crisp suits.

Fox did eventually fire Tucker, but not for his support of "great replacement" theory. Now that he's off the air on Fox, let's look at what really distinguished Tucker from the white supremacist sympathizers of the past. It was the sheer scope of his platform. Not only did he have 3 million viewers, but what he said was amplified via social media every day and around the world. It was shared in millions of daily tweets and posts and repeated in mainstream news stories. We didn't even need to watch Tucker's show to know what he was saying. The size of his reach made him even more dangerous than Bull Connor, George Wallace, or Richard Nixon.

Tucker is a very smart individual who knew exactly what he was doing—and what he was doing was making money. In the recent past, when being racist was not cool, he would have been fired for the things he said or the trauma he caused, and he would have repented, at least publicly. But the unfortunate part about Tucker is that he proved my theory that there is a value to one's soul, but he must determine what that price tag is.

*　*　*

Many people think the term "white supremacy" is overused. In fact, in conservative think tanks funded by billionaire dark money, it's considered a sign of success to be called a white supremacist when opposing diversity, equity, and inclusion initiatives, muddying the waters around critical race theory, or undermining scholar Ibram X. Kendi and his antiracist movement. If you call these people "woke," they believe they've won the prize. Perhaps that is why white supremacy is not a discussion that goes far.

In plain language, I define "white supremacy" as the belief that equality is oppression. But to go a step further, using my Tucker Carlson theory (that he used racism to advance his career and fill his pocket), you see people who we once thought had good common sense, like J. D. Vance, using white anxiety (racism) for political gain and expediency by enveloping themselves in an ideology grounded in fear of Black equality but couching it as "cancel culture."

Let's delve a little deeper. When we talk about racism, we must talk about systems in this country. Many times, people want to worry about someone calling them the N-word, but no one ever wants to get deeper into the conversation about what racism really is and how it's ingrained in our structures. You must look at the role of racism and the law. And you couple that with willful ignorance and how we teach our country's history, and you have a combustion on the issue of race, where people often steer away from having the dialogue that's necessary. I think the best example of this is when you try to have a conversation about policy and you realize that people either were not taught or are either willfully ignorant about things like Jim Crow and redlining. They didn't know about Tulsa until *Watchmen* came out on HBO. When we're examining how these policies impact people of color, you can't have sustained, substantive conversations with others who simply don't know the history.

. . .

Tucker is gone from Fox News, but it doesn't mean the harm he has caused is over. It just manifests itself in different ways. I think his firing only shows that people are tired of his bullshit and that his antics caught up with him and Fox News. And so be it. But that doesn't mean his tainted, nasty legacy is over. It's like a grape juice stain on a white couch. Even though you can get rid of most of it, the rest will always remain.

It's funny watching people rejoice over the firing of Tucker Carlson, because his legacy will never go away. He's more than just one person on the news. He's representative of the monetizing of white supremacy. It's fascinating to see that, even with his show on X, although it doesn't have the same reach, people cater to the audience that consumes Tucker as truth. That audience believes that Black people reaped some personal benefit from slavery, which on its face is utterly ignorant. They believe that enslaved Africans didn't bring skills into this country; they were taught these skills by their white slave masters, which is even more ignorant. It's that level of white supremacy that's emblematic of Tucker Carlson. And yet he gets propped up and his words get stamped with some mainstream approval—not just from white folk but even from Ice Cube and Stephen A. Smith.

. . .

It's disheartening because even though Tucker is not there, in that evening slot on Fox News, the people who will try to replace him must be just like him, if not more extreme. We don't want to believe that the white nationalism that plays to a cheering audience represents the mainstream of America. While I honestly don't believe it does, and I don't believe that all the viewers of Fox News are white nationalists, I do believe it's a large number, more than we've ever given credit to. Remember, Donald Trump got 74 million votes. It's not the majority of the nation, and it's not a silent majority, but it is a large number of people who buy into this belief that others are inferior and that for some reason white people in this country are being targeted by the LGBTQ+ community, by Black men, by so many others.

Today, whether it's country music star Jason Aldean or someone else who feels slightly persecuted because they've been called out for some ridiculous or outlandish thing they've said, they will all of a sudden protest, "You're just doing this to me because I'm white, and you don't like white people."

And that's the furthest thing from the truth. I don't dislike white people. I just hate white supremacy and those who support it.

8

THE GREAT DISTRACTION

Today, what we're up against in this country is so entrenched and deep that it demands careful examination in the light of day. We can only root it out if it's fully exposed.

"Institutional racism" is the umbrella under which capitalist racism and policy racism are sheltered. The term refers to the systemic and pervasive patterns of discrimination, bias, and disadvantage embedded within the structures, policies, and practices of our social institutions, such as government bodies, educational systems, health-care systems, and law enforcement agencies. Unlike individual acts of racism—calling someone the N-word, for example—institutional racism operates on a larger scale and affects entire groups of people based on their race or ethnicity.

Institutional racism is seen in discriminatory hiring practices, racially biased law enforcement practices, racially disparate access to quality education and health care, and the concentration of environmental hazards in economically marginalized communities. These systems and structures perpetuate and reinforce inequalities, resulting in differential treatment and outcomes for different racial or ethnic groups.

Addressing institutional racism requires acknowledging its existence, understanding its impact, and actively working toward dismantling and reforming biased policies, practices, and systems. This can involve implementing equitable policies, promoting diversity and inclusion, ensuring equal access to opportunities and resources, and engaging in anti-racist practices at all levels of society. Unfortunately, today, the efforts of our Congress and US Supreme Court are leaning the other way.

· · ·

But let's step back for a minute and recognize that there have always been periods of advancement against white supremacy, followed by periods of retrenchment.

The Reverend William Barber has observed that there have been two "reconstructions" in the United States—the one that followed the Civil War in the nineteenth century, and the one that followed the great social legislation of the 1960s, led by Dr. Martin Luther King.

Now, Reverend Barber—the cochair of the Poor People's Campaign: A National Call for Moral Revival and the founding director of the Center for Public Theology and Public Policy at Yale Divinity School—is such a forward thinker that he's even seeing the dawn of a third reconstruction.

"Even as the Constitution was being written," he told me, "racism was like a cobra under the desks of the constitutional delegates. Every time they sought to write something that might be applied to everybody, that snake would bite, and the poison would be released."

The Civil War ended in 1865, which freed the enslaved people, of course, and that was followed by the period known as Reconstruction. By the close of 1865, merely eight months after President Lincoln was gunned down by a southern white supremacist, the Thirteenth Amendment was ratified, which legally ended the scourge of slavery. In 1868, the Fourteenth Amendment granted citizenship to Black Americans and equal civil rights for all persons—not just for all citizens, but for everyone.

By 1870, the Fifteenth Amendment guaranteed the right to vote to men, prohibiting both the federal and all state governments from "denying" or—importantly—"abridging" anyone from doing so based on "race, color, or previous condition of servitude." It's not that you couldn't just deny someone the right to vote, you couldn't *abridge* it—you couldn't throw obstacles in their way, you couldn't block any bridge to vote.

Five years later, we had the Civil Rights Act of 1875, which protected "all citizens in their civil and legal rights" and specifically provided for "equal treatment in public accommodations and public transportation" and prohibited exclusion from jury service.

Wait just a moment, you might say. Weren't these exactly the civil rights that activists fought for in the 1950s and 1960s? As a matter of fact, they were, because in 1883 the Civil Rights Act was overruled by the US Supreme Court, green-lighting nearly a century of post–Civil War Jim Crow laws.

"If you think about that," Reverend Barber said, "this means that by 1875, we had everything that we then had to turn around and pass again in 1964. At the March on Washington in 1963, one hundred years after the passage of the Emancipation Proclamation, Dr. King pointed out this very fact, basically saying this makes no sense."

Ten years after the end of the Civil War, every state legislature in the South was controlled by a diverse coalition—or, as Reverend Barber calls it, a "Fusion" coalition—that had wrested postwar power away from white Confederates. By 1870, every southern state legislature had revised its constitution to prohibit slavery, to guarantee that Black men (though not yet women) could vote, and to outlaw white supremacist organizations like the Ku Klux Klan. And in that year, Hiram Revels, a Black man and Republican, was elected to be a US senator from Mississippi. Black representatives began serving in the US Congress as well. But in 1876, all of this began to unravel.

The presidential election that year was incredibly close, and a consensus candidate who had lost the popular vote, Rutherford B. Hayes, struck a deal with the South: Award to me your Electoral College votes, and I'll pull all federal troops out of the southern states. In other words, grant me the presidency, and y'all can go back to the way you always did your business. Reverend Barber half-jokingly dubs it "making America great again in 1877."

This kicked open the stable doors, enabling the rise of the Red Shirts and the KKK. Jim Crow laws were passed all throughout the South. White supremacists went after voting rights, they went after the courts, and they began to utilize the criminal justice system as a way of retrenching southern Black men, who were no longer technically slaves, into lives that closely resembled the miseries of slavery. For example, Black men would be arrested on any manner of trumped-up charges and rented as "prisoners" to former plantation owners. By the 1890s, almost all the majority and powerful Black and white coalitions of the South had been overturned. The voting turnout of Blacks went from as high as 90 percent in some southern states to 5 percent or less. By 1896, the Supreme Court held, in the notorious case of *Plessy v. Ferguson*, that "separate but equal" facilities and accommodations are in fact constitutional, which effectively overturned all the work of Reconstruction.

Then came our country's first coup d'état, in Wilmington, North Carolina, where duly elected Black and white "Fusionists" in a biracial government were run out of office by the barrel of a gun. Property and businesses owned by Black citizens were destroyed, including the city's only Black newspaper, and up to three hundred people were killed.

As Reverend Barber tells it: "They sent telegrams from Wilmington, saying, 'This is how we take back America. This is how we restore the country to the rights known to the white man.' What followed were many different insurrections and riots around the country. Black men were being hung almost every week, sometimes more than every week."

In 1912, the Democrat Woodrow Wilson was elected president of the United States and turned his back on the Black community. Wilson undermined the employment of Blacks in the federal government. He brought the racist movie *Birth of a Nation* to the White House and had his entire cabinet view it in the West Wing. Arguably Hollywood's first blockbuster hit, this is a film that glorifies the Klan and portrays Black politicians during Reconstruction as buffoons and fools. President Wilson had a record of racist writings, including the reflection that "white men were roused by an instinct of mere self-preservation until at last there had sprung into existence a great Ku Klux Klan, a veritable empire of the South to protect the Southern country."

By 1919, following a great migration of Blacks from the South, so much Black blood was spilling in dozens of northern American cities from white supremacist terrorism and racial riots that NAACP secretary James Weldon Johnson called it the Red Summer. Of course, all these racial attacks continued nationwide, straight through the mid-twentieth century, shocking the Black community with the death of a child, Emmett Till, in 1955 at the hands of members of a local police force. All of this led directly to a second reconstruction, beginning with Rosa Parks and the Montgomery bus boycott, encompassing the movement of Dr. King, and concluding with the passage of the great civil rights legislation of the mid-1960s—much of which, as can be anticipated in view of this country's history, is currently being chipped away.

"When we say the rise of white supremacy," Reverend Barber told me, "I like to say it's not that we're having a rise of white supremacy—we keep having reiterations of it, keep having various ebbs and flows. And the reason, I believe, is that we've never really dealt with racism. Ibram X. Kendi, who wrote *Stamped from the Beginning*, observed that we make a fundamental error, even today, in talking about race, because we act as though race came first, and then racism grew out of race. In other words, first people don't like you because of your race, the color of your skin, and therefore they create racism. Actually, though, it's the racism that came first, the decision to have a certain people disenfranchised for other people's economic and political benefits."

The systems, the policies, and much of our political and social culture is born out of racism—not race. Once you decide you want to have all the money, once you decide you want to have all the political power, then you look around and ask, Who do we have to oppress selectively in order to do that?

The Prescription

"One of the mistakes I think we got to stop making today is if we're going to deal with racism, and white supremacy, it's not just rising up when we see overt racism, like saying the N-word or some *Sesame Street* characters aren't speaking to young girls," says Reverend Barber. "What we have to do is analyze what racism is today in *policy*, because the truth of the matter is, the overt racism we see is actually a distraction—people are missing the racist *policies*."

In other words, too often we fail to call out the racism in legislative policy. Here's an example: the Voting Rights Act of 1965, possibly the crowning achievement of both Dr. King and the Johnson administration, was gutted in 2013—roughly the same period of time as between the passage of the Thirteenth, Fourteenth, and Fifteenth Amendments and the *Plessy v. Ferguson* "separate but equal" decision a hundred-some years before. And today we sit here in America with less voting rights protection than we had in 1965 after the Voting Rights Act was ratified. That's racism.

"If you think about it," Reverend Barber pointed out, "when that law was gutted, you didn't see mass protests in the street. Now, if the police shot someone Black, you would have—and rightfully so. But if we limit our opposition to that, we're disabling our ability to really change racism, because how do those . . . chiefs of police and sheriffs get into a place to protect those officers who act in a racist manner to kill unarmed Black people? Through the political process."

Here's a second example: today we have 140 million poor and low-wealth people in this country, people who are below or near the poverty level. That's 43 percent of the nation, 52 percent of our children, and it includes 66 million white people along with 26 million Blacks—but that's 60.9 percent of all Black people. Poverty is created by policy: the denial of health care, the denial of living wages, the fact that we hadn't raised the minimum wage for twelve years—all of which would have lifted some 41 percent of Blacks out of poverty. So why isn't that called racism?

Reverend Barber cites studies that show some seven hundred people a day die from poverty. "So," he said, "if 60.9 percent of Black people are in poverty, and seven hundred people die from poverty, that's a quarter million people a year. That means more people die from policies that racially impact Black people than from police brutality. And yet we don't tend to call inequitable policies violent?"

Coretta Scott King once said that violence was not just a racist shooting her husband. She argued that violence is denying people a living wage, denying them health care, denying them education, denying them their culture. An apathetic attitude that refuses to address these other forms of violence is in fact violence as well, she believed.

"When we talk about the rise of white supremacy," Reverend Barber continued, "we must expand that to include the racist policy impact. If we only talk about white supremacy in terms of white supremacist groups, I believe we actually disable our ability to truly deal with it. Historically, what one finds behind the violence of racism are policy-driven actions. The Klan was a political organization that didn't just hate Blacks because of their color. They loved power. They knew that racist policies empowered them."

Dr. King once asserted that the greatest fear of the southern aristocrat and the racist politician was the coming together of the masses of poor Blacks and poor whites into a political power bloc that could fundamentally shift the economic architecture of race. So, in light of Reverend Barber's observations, why didn't we more strongly call out as racist someone like Senator Mitch McConnell for stacking the Supreme Court with judges who have systematically dismantled many of the progressive civil rights–era accomplishments?

When Trump says there are "very fine people on both sides," or when a US senator from Alabama nonchalantly suggests that white nationalists are people who hold "a few probably different beliefs," and such quotes are blown up by the media (social and otherwise), they are actually distracting us from much more significant and hard-core institutional, capitalist, and policy racism. Meanwhile, the Supreme Court fills up with white men raised by groups like the Federalist Society, and white supremacy reaps what was sowed: restrictions

on the Voting Rights Act, an overturning of women's reproductive rights, a weakening of Miranda rights, and an evis-
ceration of affirmative action. And this rollback of civil rights
protections obviously does not benefit Black Americans.

* * *

Reverend Barber sees at the foundation of contemporary
white supremacy an intersection of five interlocking injustices: systemic racism, poverty, environmental disparity, the
war economy, and a distorted moral view of Christian nationalism.

Reverend Barber has insisted to me many times that we
have to find a way to build a broad fusion coalition of Black,
white, Brown, Native, and Asian folk. Poor people now represent 30 percent of the electorate overall—and 45 percent of
the electorate in battleground states—and the demographics
are shifting. This is one reason for the rise now in white supremacist policies (or Trumpism or Making America Great
Again or whatever you want to call it). As they said in South
Africa toward the end of apartheid, a dying mule kicks the
hardest.

The first thing we must address is systemic racism—not
just race but systemic policy racism, voter suppression, and
mass incarceration. We must address that racism in terms
of how it impacts Black people, Brown people, First Nation
people, and Asians. And we must expose the collateral damage done to white people. For instance, the current racist
voter suppression laws that are being passed today, mostly
in southern states, will deny 55 million people the access to
the polls that they had in 2020—not just Black people but

55 million Americans of all races. While voter suppression is targeted at Blacks, the actual impact of it on women and college students and young people is much broader.

We also must address the problem of poverty. We cannot have a sustainable society where 43 percent of the world's wealthiest country is living in poverty. Health-care costs are contributing to the problem. We can't say we're addressing racism and white supremacy and have a nation where 87 million people are either uninsured or underinsured, and more than two thousand people a day are dying in families without affordable health-care access.

Added to this, we must address environmental deprivation, because poor Black and Brown folk are the ones most hurt when factories and other potentially hazardous industries are placed in their communities, which they disproportionately are.

Then we have to address the war economy and the militarization of our communities. The United States currently spends fifty-four cents of every discretionary dollar in the federal budget on the military, an enormous source of funds that flow directly to military contractors. A one-year military contract at, say, Boeing could fund all the people that have been denied health care in the southern states because of a continued refusal to expand Medicaid. The majority of people who would be helped by the Affordable Care Act are southern whites, but they either can't see, or are distracted from seeing, this reality. (The Affordable Care Act is called Obamacare, by the way, because it's branded through a racial lens.)

The last of Reverend Barber's five interlocking injustices is the inexorable attempt to sanctify white supremacy as a religion or as a religious morality. Christian nationalism seeks to merge religious beliefs with political power, potentially undermining the principles of separation of church and state. When religious ideology becomes intertwined with governance, it diminishes the principles of religious freedom and individual liberties that are essential to a healthy democracy. In some instances, Christian nationalist movements are also associated with attempts to suppress the rights of marginalized groups, such as LGBTQ+ individuals, women seeking reproductive rights, and religious minorities.

In Reverend Barber's words: "We have to challenge these five interlocking injustices with an intergenerational, interracial, intersectional fusion movement in the streets, in the political suites, at the ballot box, and in the pulpit, and we have to do it without economic power. Dr. King always said that it couldn't be Black people alone; it has to be a diverse coalition."

*   *   *

Spanning the Civil War and the civil rights eras, this country has experienced two reconstructions followed by a white supremacist pushback against each. Reverend Barber believes from the depth of his heart that we're entering a third reconstruction period. He's experiencing it:

Our movement is bringing white folk from Appalachia in West Virginia together with Black folk from Alabama on the common ground of poverty. I say the same thing in East Kentucky that I say in the mountains of Appalachia—I don't change a thing. And amazingly, we have found an audience among those folks because they start understanding they're being played too. I was in East Kentucky, in so-called Hatfield and McCoy country. We all went up there, and people are saying, "They're gonna kill you." I said, no, because we got some good people up there too.

We went up on a Tuesday, some five hundred people showed up, mostly white, along with some Black folk up from Louisville. I put a chart up on the board and said, "I want to start out talking about race." And when it got kind of quiet, I said, "Let's look at all the state legislators that have told you that there's cheating in the elections and we need to pull back on voting rights because of flaws." Then, I said, "Okay, here's the list of all the legislators in Kentucky that vote for racist voter suppression laws. Here's all the legislators in your state that claim we need to end affirmative action. Now"—and I paused—"let's go look at all the legislators in your state that also vote against unions in the coal mines and vote against raising wages." Suddenly, this white man stands up and says, "Do that again." And so I did. "Damn," he exclaimed, "they playing us against each other!"

Reverend Barber spoke for two hours to these Kentuckians from five solid red counties. One man told him, "The Democrats stopped coming back here, and the Republicans hardly come either, but when they do come, they lie and try to divide the folk. It's not even a red county. Most of the folks here don't even vote."

The media doesn't report on any of this because they

only want to talk about race when there's a killing or when a teacher calls somebody the N-word in the classroom. But that's not really what racism is. Hard-core racism is policy racism, and the antics of name-calling are generated to create divisions in society and to obscure what's happening in legislative policy.

"We have to go after the policy," Reverend Barber insists. "The prophets in the Bible challenged the king. They challenged the injustices. We must protest over policy, and not just unjust killings. The slaves didn't just want freedom. They wanted citizenship. When the NAACP silently marched in the early 1900s, that was over the policy of lynching. What drew us in the streets of Selma to protest voter suppression was the murder of Jimmie Lee Jackson by an Alabama state trooper. Rosa Parks sparked the bus boycott, and we brought down the entire Jim Crow system of public segregation because of what they did to Emmett Till. We got to define murder as bigger than just killing an individual—we must see the policy murders, the policies that kill thousands. If folks—Black, white, Brown, Asian, everyone—could see this, it will change how people vote; it would change everything."

*　*　*

Let's consider one last phenomenon by way of illustrating the policy racism argument—the election of President Obama and the backlash that followed, in part in the form of Trumpism. Obama was nominated on August 28, 2008—the anniversary of both the murder of Emmett Till and the March on Washington. Why were some people so scared of Obama? What was it that made them freak out and even seek to deny his American citizenship? On the surface, the easy answer is that he is a Black man.

But let's examine how Obama actually won (the same general path, by the way, that President Biden later traveled). He pierced the Republican stranglehold on the southern and southwestern states that had been forged by Ronald Reagan and essentially surrendered for generations by the Democratic Party. Obama developed a Black, white, Brown, and Asian coalition that for the first time in years delivered to the Democrats certain southern states. He broke through the illusion that the South was forever lost to Democrats.

So why are legislators in North Carolina now campaigning to weaken the Voting Rights Act? The reason Obama won that state is because of early voting—that's what put him over the top. And that's exactly what the southern states are now trying to curtail, with some, like Florida, doing so successfully. When did we first start hearing about voter suppression laws? In 2009, after Obama's election.

We can't just say that white supremacists and their sympathizers hated Obama because he's Black. No, you've got to go deeper. As Reverend Barber so insightfully points out, first came racism, and then came race. The supporters of white supremacist philosophy—whether they be Donald Trump, Jesse Watters, Megyn Kelly, Mitch McConnell, or others—want to maintain all the power. They don't want equity or equality. They want to maintain their power and privilege.

And they know that carefully coordinated, strategic racist communications and policies have always worked in America.

9

THE UNTAPPED POWER
OF BLACK MEN

I'm often asked why I ran for office. When I think about it, the answer is simple. I didn't run for office to be popular on Instagram or to be grand marshal of the Dogwood Parade in Denmark, South Carolina. I was only seventeen years old when I started thinking about running for the state House of Representatives. As a student at Morehouse College, partying hard and nearly failing my freshman semester, I got the political bug after interning in Jim Clyburn's office. I felt a calling to try to make a difference in my small hometown. Four years later, in 2005, the same year I graduated and the summer before I was headed to law school, I told my parents I was going to run for office. On September 18, the day I turned twenty-one, I announced my candidacy against Thomas Rhoad, an eighty-something white man who had reigned over a Black district for twenty-five years but had really done nothing for it.

All I had were six "Sellers for House" T-shirts, a couple of pairs of dress pants, one pair of shoes, a little bit of Facebook, no Instagram, no Twitter, and no Snapchat, but I pounded the pavement because I was dead serious about wanting to change Denmark; I wanted to make my mom and dad proud too, and I wanted to fulfill the legacy of those who came before me.

I enjoyed knocking on doors, and I loved walking up to a double-wide, the ones with a long dirt yard in front. At places like that, you never knew if you were going to be greeted with a smile or a rottweiler.

Today, there's a lot of fame and celebrity associated with politics. And though I'm still a young man, things were very different when I got started because local elected officials were damn sure not famous, and they were not social media influencers. This was prior to the widespread use of social media in politics. It was prior to the mass text messages from candidates who want you to vote for them.

I didn't want fame. I ran because I wanted to change the way people got health care, to build new schools in my hometown, to repair roads, to fix the water in Denmark, to put people to work; I wanted to raise the minimum wage and take down a confederate flag. I wasn't jaded by reality yet, and I didn't understand how difficult those challenges were going to be.

At the age of twenty-two, I became the youngest-ever member of the South Carolina House of Representatives, but I don't believe anybody would tell you that my election in 2006, in Bamberg County, was a watershed moment (that wouldn't have been politically or historically accurate). But what my political race did do was create a ripple effect. It made headlines. And it showed that you could be a young Black man with dreams and vision, with only an iota of political talent, and still be able to serve in the upper echelons of government.

Before then, we didn't see young Black male politicians like me throughout the country. At that time, Barack Obama was a phenomenon from the 2004 Democratic National Convention speech, but he wasn't yet the Barack Obama that we eventually came to know. After my win in 2006, you began to see young Black men run for city and state offices. You saw them emerging on the national stage, and you even saw them working in the halls of the US government, such as Maxwell Frost, the first member of Gen Z to be elected to Congress, and my friend Antjuan Seawright, who has advised the likes of Hakeem Jeffries, Jim Clyburn, and Hillary Clinton.

By no means do I take credit for any of that, but my campaign managed to knock a small crack in the glass ceiling. More people began to think young Black men had a role to play in American politics.

* * *

I met Antjuan Seawright a few years after my election. It was during the 2008 presidential primary; I was a surrogate for Barack Obama, and he was a staffer for Hillary Clinton. We didn't really get to know each other until after the election when we crossed paths again in the halls of the South Carolina State House in Columbia. At that time, he was an aide for Senator Darrell Jackson, and I was still a legislator.

Now a Democratic strategist, businessman, and political correspondent, Antjuan is a success, but there's no metric in this country that would have predicted it. The grandson of a sharecropper, he emerged like me from the dirt roads of South

Carolina, from Swansea, a town of around eight hundred people. He's country as hell, his sayings and colloquialisms are legendary in DC, and he speaks with a twang, but his words are truthful. And although he's only thirty-eight, he has the spirit and soul of a seventy-year-old man.

What's special about Antjuan is that he's an example of not only what Black men can be, but what we can and should do for each other. He has found a place among a new wave of Black millennial male political voices constantly warning the Democrats to take the power of Black male voters seriously—or else.

*   *   *

Antjuan and I and other Black men in the party often say, "Democrats must meet Black men where they are." So what does that look like? If Antjuan is answering the question, there is no doubt he will always repeat some version of this: "We Democrats need to meet Black men where Barack Obama found them, at the spades card table, the barbershops, the horseshoe tables, the holes-in-the-wall, the gyms, at the car wash, the fraternity meetings, after church, before church."

In Antjuan's case, he's not just talking out of the side of his mouth. A year prior to the 2024 election, he visited four barbershops in Milwaukee and Mississippi to engage Black male voters on behalf of the Democratic National Committee. This is an example of how intentional and purposeful we must be. For far too long, the playbook for older white progressives was to pay us no attention until Labor Day of the year of the election, which is too late. Politicians can no longer just show up at a high school football game on a Friday night or a fish fry at a church on Sunday.

And what "meeting Black men where they are" *doesn't* mean is showing up and telling them what's important to them. Rather, we must show up to listen, so that they can tell us what's important. If we don't listen, we're going to continue to see the whittling away of the Black male vote.

* * *

The Waffle House is one of the best places to do the work because it's where you can talk with people from every walk of life, including rich white people. "That's what you call focus groups," Antjuan says. He listens and learns in Walmart and lunches at the Lizard's Thicket, Kiki's Chicken and Waffles, Big T's Bar-B-Que, all of the restaurants in the Midlands of South Carolina. In those places, he gets his fill of what he calls "polling and political education."

After the 2016 election, Democrats learned a hard lesson. We saw something unfortunate happening with a very important constituency. We noticed there was real erosion taking place among Black men who normally voted for Democrats. And so, Black men like Antjuan and me started to sound the alarm about this issue.

We began to repeat this message to the party: "We Democrats may pride ourselves on the network of the Black vote, but the collective Black vote is where we have always found strength. We've not only been the nurse to the party but one of the great arteries of this country. That could all change if the party takes its eyes off the ball."

Truth is, there is a disconnect between the Democratic Party—which has historically spoken to the needs and concerns of Black men—and what's being communicated today.

And what is being communicated to us is that we are not important, that we can be ignored and taken for granted.

Black men all around the nation are telling us that several things have turned them away from voting for the Democratic Party. They say the Democrats are not fighting enough and that the party does not give a damn about Black men; they only care about Black women.

What's happened is that over the years people who don't look like us or don't have our shared values have tried to split our community into two, attempting to make us think it's one or the other: Black men or Black women. But historically, we've always found strength in the collective Black vote as Black men and Black women. Every major civil rights movement in this country has been led by Black men on the front lines, with Black women beside them helping to lead the charge.

My dad talks constantly about the Black women of the civil rights era, the "sheroes" who were extremely important but often left out of the history books. But let's not forget Black men were dying and putting themselves on the line, being sacrificed and hanged right before our eyes—and at rates we'd never seen before.

During a recent conversation with Antjuan, I said, "Seawright, there are people on K Street who believe Black men only care about things like criminal justice and social justice issues."

"True," said Antjuan. "But we know . . . that elections are not won on K Street; they are won on our streets."

He's right. The Democratic Party must understand that African American men are not a monolith. We care about the things that every constituency cares about. We care about health care, education, a clean and safe environment, access to capital, and entrepreneurship. We care about what the judicial benches at both the federal and local levels look like, and we care about voting rights, access to the internet, and infrastructure.

"We also care about all those issues that tend to be generational issues," Antjuan said, "and maybe that's where the disconnect is."

In every election since 2016, Democrats have seen at least a 1 percent erosion of the Black male vote. And the size of the Black male erosion vote could grow as the electorate in this country continues to expand, with the browning of America happening right before our eyes, and as the educated generation of Black folk, including Black men, becomes more engaged because the actions of extremists are forcing us to do so. That means more Black and Brown people who normally vote for Democrats will be more critical and hyperfocused on what the Democrats are or are not doing to earn their votes and trust.

"We got a lot of work to do," Antjuan said to me. "And we have to do it quick because we can have 100 percent turnout among Black women, but if we don't have enough Black men turning out for Democrats, the party of the values that most of us line up with will lose."

In Antjuan's view, "the white man should potentially qualify for the Lifetime Achievement Award at the NAACP Awards every year, because they figured out that if they can pit Black women against Black men, they can not only divide our community, from a divide-and-conquer perspective, but they can also grab ahold of the power switch for a very long time in this country."

Jim Clyburn often says that what we've seen before, we will see again, and we've seen people try this before, coming into our communities and creating divisions. Frederick Douglass, a former slave and great abolitionist, wrote about the old divide-and-conquer trap in his autobiography. The slave masters created divisions by allowing some slaves to work in the big house while others struggled and toiled under the blazing sun for hours.

If we are not careful about the intense trickery that's happening now to divide us, our issues can easily slip to the back burner. Other things are happening, including the expansion of the Latino vote, that will capture the attention of the national parties. I subscribe to the political adage that if you're not at the table, you're probably on the menu.

The fact is, if we don't win elections, and if our voices are not heard and organized both before the election and at the ballot box, we will always be on the menu and our issues will be lost.

* * *

Latino men and Black men are almost in the same boat. We've seen a similar erosion happening with Latino men increasingly voting for Republicans, but Black Americans have so much to lose if we don't go to the polls together—or at all. The scariest development is the rise of the nonvoter because an unmotivated, uncast vote for Democrats is like a vote for the right-wing extremists who want to ban books and whitewash history and who think it's okay to call Black folk "colored" in 2024 and to say that white nationalists are not necessarily racist.

Black Americans are still the most powerful voting bloc in the nation, which is why right-wing extremists are trying to divide us. If they succeed, we are in more danger than we could ever imagine. Very recent history shows what happens when they have their hand on the power switch: not only do they put ultraconservatives on the US Supreme Court but they load up the lower courts with conservative judges as well. And those judges render decisions that will keep us on life support in our community for three or four generations and that will cause our ancestors to tremble in their graves.

We've always believed, as Black folk, that every generation gets better, stronger, wiser, and more stable. But now, the right wing has transformed the Supreme Court into a heartless machine, and the attacks against progressivism in America have caused a persistent ache, a throbbing pain that likely won't go away for a very long time. Whether we are talking about affirmative action or *Roe v. Wade*, the Supreme Court majority has targeted groups of people who traditionally vote Democrat. What the courts really did, Antjuan said to me, "was roll back decades of precedents to appease a few residents in this country."

"Let's go even deeper," I suggested. "If you look back at history, starting with the Civil Rights Act of 1964, every time Black people experienced progress in this country, we've been met with extreme backlash."

Antjuan agreed and offered several examples. President Carter made transformational appointments, including hiring the first Black division head of the Department of Justice and the first Black ambassador to the United Nations, but this was followed by Reagan's war on drugs. It's hard to imagine today that millions of Black and Latino Americans were being criminalized for their addictions, but that is what Ronald Reagan did. In the larger scheme of things, his harsh prison sentences took many Black men out of their households and disenfranchised them, making it nearly impossible for them to go to college or get bank loans. In fact, it would not be incorrect to say that Reagan's war on drugs was the first modern-day step to deconstructing and crippling the Black family. George Bush Sr. continued the war on drugs and appointed conservative Clarence Thomas to the Supreme Court.

Then we got Bill Clinton, the young, handsome, progressive but pragmatic white governor from Little Rock, Arkansas, who changed the game for Black people across the country. Under Clinton, African American unemployment dropped, and our median household income rose by 25 percent; Black people finally started to build the wealth that we'd never had before. We started to get insurance policies, and we started going to college at higher rates after 1992.

Then, another Bush took over the White House, but we responded by electing Barack Obama, and then of course there was backlash against Obama for giving us health care, and that backlash was Donald Trump, the Tea Party, the white nationalists, and all the other things that come with extremism. The backlash today is more sophisticated and extreme. And unlike in the past, we have not been able to bounce back. "In fact," Antjuan said, "we have not been able to put a stop plug to the renewed effort of white nationalism in this country since Trump. Unfortunately, the Biden election did not do that."

We can't blame the wearing away of the Black male vote strictly on Black men feeling overshadowed by Black women. Disinformation campaigns in 2016 and 2020 specifically targeted Black Americans, especially Black men, who will likely be the target again in future presidential elections. With the rise of AI, experts warn that the disinformation campaigns will be more sophisticated than ever before.

A Senate report found that Russian operatives working for the Kremlin-backed Internet Research Agency (IRA) concentrated their efforts on the nation's racial problems, saturating Black and Latin American voters with fake messages during the 2016 elections. The investigators noted: "No single group of Americans was targeted by the IRA information operation more than African Americans. By far, race and related issues were the preferred target of the information warfare campaign designed to divide the country in 2016."

The *Guardian* claimed that Trump's 2016 campaign pinpointed 3.5 million African American voters with disinformation about Hillary Clinton. Trump's goal was to make us so annoyed and frustrated that we'd stay home from the polls. In 2020, not only did many Black men stay home but Trump took 19 percent of the Black male vote, an increase from 13 percent in 2016. The Senate investigators believe that misinformation and disinformation targeting Black men is partially to blame.

Antjuan heard from leaders who attended the Senate briefings that Black men often entangle themselves in disinformation by entering the dark web, but believe me, the dark web isn't the only place Black men are being targeted.

In 2022, Keisha Lance Bottoms, the former Atlanta mayor who was advising Biden at the time, told MSNBC host Jonathan Capehart that Black men were targets of misinformation leading up to the midterm election. Capehart then showed an MSNBC clip of Stacey Abrams, then a Georgia Democratic gubernatorial nominee, who said basically the same thing.

However, the Black host seemed to wonder out loud if Abrams might simply be disgruntled. Was Abrams getting "the Black support she needs in her race against Brian Kemp?" he asked.

Keisha went straight to the point. "Listen, Jonathan, I think that Stacey is spot-on. I listen as my kids watch NBA highlights and whatever else they watch on YouTube. I hear the misinformation being piped in. My twelve-year-old, my fourteen-year-old son, my twenty-year-old is getting it."

The former mayor makes a point I am sure many people miss, that misinformation often comes from seemingly safe places—a popular podcaster, a YouTuber, or a TikTok personality—but I am going to go a little deeper. Many people mistakenly believe there's a Russian disinformation farm or some racist white man behind every sinister ploy to diminish Black male voter empowerment, but that's simply not the case.

Sometimes, it's people who look like us—the Ice Cubes of the world, the Stephen A. Smiths, the Jason Whitlocks—Black men who willingly disseminate disinformation and misinformation just to receive a hug from white conservatives. Why do it? I don't know, but they remind me of Samuel L. Jackson's character hugging Leonardo DiCaprio's cruel slave plantation owner in *Django Unchained*.

I've often said that the cruelest trick that America played

on Black folk was replacing Thurgood Marshall with Clarence Thomas. We don't need to get into the judicial depth of either man; I think that's been well noted. Plus, Black conservatism, particularly among African American men, is nothing new. In fact, some of our greatest scholars had more than a streak of conservatism. Today, however, we can draw a direct line from Clarence Thomas to some of our newer media voices, like those I've mentioned above, who take a bombastic, anti-intellectual approach to propping up right-wing propaganda, usually coddling the likes of Tucker Carlson or Will Cain.

Black men have always been very diverse and dynamic, but now we're seeing a new streak of entrepreneurial conservatism that allows individuals to be bombastic, lacking any depth while shouldering the burden of white extremism for clicks or views—or simply the white gaze. Instead of putting their shoulder to the wheel and being concerned about the plight of those who look like them, these Black men are inspired by the thesis of Bill Cosby's infamous "pound cake speech." For those of you who have no idea what I'm talking about, let's go back to 2004. During the NAACP Legal Defense Fund awards ceremony, Cosby gave a speech, or rather a tirade, criticizing African Americans, especially poor Black people. He blamed us for everything, including the way we speak, single parenthood, things we spend our own money on, and lack of respectability.

Looking at the incarcerated, these are not political criminals. These are people going around stealing Coca-Cola. People getting shot in the back of the head over a piece of pound cake! And then we all run out and are outraged, "The cops shouldn't have shot him." What the hell was he doing with the pound cake in his hand? I wanted a piece of pound cake just as bad as anybody else, and I looked at it and I had no money. And something called parenting said, "If you get caught with it, you're going to embarrass your mother." Not "You're going to get your butt kicked." No. "You're going to embarrass your family."

Cosby continued with this diatribe for several years, tearing through Black parenting and stereotyping Black men for "beating their women" and "not wanting a job."

The new breed of conservative entrepreneurs likes to take slices of the "pound cake speech" and combine it with a shallow understanding of complex policy positions, such as affirmative action or student loans. And then they go on TV and help assuage their white counterparts' guilt. Sadly, this has brought on a set of newer and louder conservative Black men who follow the same messed-up blueprint of Stephen A. Smith and Jason Whitlock. I won't name them here because I don't want to waste ink on them. Although when they do stumble across these pages, they will surely take to X or Threads or Instagram and play victim because hit dogs, of course, will holler.

I don't want to take away from the traditional conservative values and moral ethos of people like Tim Scott, Shermichael Singleton, and Michael Steele, who, for all intents and purposes, believe that conservative values best prop up and move forward Black and Brown folk. We may have different views on policies, but I'd never question their morals or ethics, which are the opposite of those of the Black men who prop up white supremacy for entertainment value and followers.

Are they really doing it for the clicks? Truth is, I am still not sure why they crave the white gaze so much, but I would love for the early 1990s Ice Cube to write a rap about today's Ice Cube. I would love the Winston-Salem alums to critique the Stephen A. Smith of today.

Smith, Cube, and Whitlock have become a staple of misinformation and disinformation. That they crave attention so much that they will push out half-truths and lies about Black men proves one very important truth: The situation we are in is far more complex than we thought. It's a conundrum that we must be strong and push back against, whether the lies are coming from Russia or from our own.

The Prescription

Yes, Black men are targeted by people we love, targeted by law enforcement, and even targeted by people from a whole other country. Are we targeted because we're weak? The answer is no. Are we targeted because we're susceptible? The answer probably is yes. But why is that? As I have been saying over and over, you've got to peel back the layers of the onion and ask yourself why. Why do people feel they can target Black men for election interference? Why do people feel they can target Black men to monetize misogyny?

The answer is simple. If a group of individuals (in this case Black men) is neglected, is not shown love by their own country and society as a whole, not paid attention to, then a certain vulnerable portion of that group will gravitate toward the people who *are* talking to them. They will allow that void to be filled with misinformation, disinformation, misogyny, hate, and bigotry. As a result, some of the individuals we care about, the Black men we love but neglected, are being filled with bullshit.

. . .

While we have the ostentatious buffoons on the scene who show up every two to four years, doing nothing to help Black men or the culture, we also have a new generation of young Black elected officials who are helping, including Antonio Delgado, the former rapper turned lieutenant governor of New York; Atlanta mayor Andre Dickens; Florida congressman Maxwell Frost; Birmingham mayor Randall Woodfin; and Little Rock mayor Frank Scott Jr. There's also New York congressmen Jamaal Bowman, Ritchie Torres, and Hakeem Jeffries.

These Black men are the prescription, the answer to filling that void. We must throw a spotlight on them, show them the support they need, and hold them up so that more Black men can see them as inspirations and hear them speak to their core.

To some extent, these men are all throwbacks to the past— throwbacks to Martin Luther King and Clarence Jones and Ralph David Abernathy—in the way that they carry themselves with such style. Whether they are rocking Afros or bald heads, beards or clean-shaven faces, T-shirts or custom-made suits, they move like the giants of yesterday. They are fearless, like Representative Ritchie Torres, who has become known for his fight against anti-Semitism, or Michigan lieutenant governor Garlin Gilchrist, who evolved into one of the leaders during COVID.

These are not cases of style over substance. It's clear these brothers are intelligent from the moment they open their mouths and well prepared for anything, whether it's enticing corporations to relocate to their districts or getting in the well of a Black church and taking the audience to new places with depth and excitement and cadence.

Think about the two Justins: Justin Pearson and Justin Jones, the two young Black legislators in Nashville. Back in 2022, the Republican-controlled House of Representatives in Tennessee tried to expel them when they rallied for gun restrictions after six people were killed in a school shooting. With fists in the air, they harkened back to a time when people were truly public servants and not just politicians.

All these men share three unique characteristics. First, they're young, in their twenties, thirties, and forties. Second, none of them get caught up in the hype of being a celebrity. They're not trying to be on the next iteration of *Love and Hip Hop*. Instead, they're trying to be legends in their own right, earning that title by being the best public servants they can be. And finally, their ability to be articulate on a variety of subjects, to succeed in their unique environments, is the perfect antidote to the empty suits I've already discussed. These men all have a core, a core that speaks to real issues, that speaks to the future, a core that says, "This is also what Black men can do."

. . .

It sucks all the air out of the room like a vacuum when you hear white conservatives, evangelicals, or conservative media pundits talk about Black-on-Black crime, asking why we don't care about Black folk killing Black folk. Or why we don't care about struggling cities like Chicago or Baltimore. These red herrings imply that we don't have pain from watching fourteen- or fifteen-year-old Black children kill themselves or innocent bystanders, that we don't recognize the systemic underpinnings of why we live in communities where violence is so prevalent, and that we don't see how ignoring the degradation causes the violence to bubble up.

I must be honest: I'm tired—I am so tired of paying for funerals. I don't want to wake up again and learn about the murder of a rapper like King Von or Takeoff of Migos or of so many unnamed individuals who are not hip-hop superstars. And yes, I'm tired of seeing the names of our dead on a T-shirt. But we must explore the systemic issues, and we must dispel the notion that there is such a thing as Black-on-Black crime, because there's not. We simply live in highly segregated communities. We all live in communities where crimes are perpetrated on individuals who look like us. And so yes, most of the crime perpetrated against white folk is committed by other white folk, and most of the crime perpetrated against Black people is committed by other Black people. That's just very basic sociology, but people don't care about facts these days. Instead, they want to treat Black men as hypermasculine, toxic beasts who can't control themselves.

What we must do is peel back the layers of years of oppression, degradation, disrespect, and disregard for the ills of Black men, even as Black men tried to lift up an era ravaged by Jim Crow or devastated by crack cocaine, and even as we carried our families and communities on our backs. We have to examine how Black men have continued to be devalued in the political process while we continued to lift up leaders like Joe Biden and Hillary Clinton.

Black men have had to do these things for the party, for our community, and for America, and all while society expects and wants us to fail. Even today, young Black boys who can't dribble a basketball or rap have too few paths to make it out of poverty. We must begin to have these serious discussions and find ways to help Black men lift themselves and their families up and out of bondage as they have lifted up and built this country.

* * *

Two of the virtues that people underestimate about Black men are our strength and our resilience. We see individuals who have come from intense environments where the saying "Pressure bursts pipes or makes diamonds" is very true.

As Black men, we have no choice but to succeed; we can't fail our mothers, our families, or ourselves; we can't fail our communities. The pressure that the world puts on us, and that we put on ourselves, is fracturing for some Black men. We must do our job as a community to rebuild and heal those the pressure has gotten to.

But for other Black men, the pressure turns them into diamonds. That doesn't mean everybody is going to be the CEO of a company. In fact, some Black men are going to be there every Tuesday and Friday to pick up your trash. They're going to make sure they take care of their families, that they attend the parent-teacher conferences, and that they love their wives and their children.

I tell people all the time that we are the backbones of our communities. And although we feel this immense pressure, Black men have a great deal of strength and power, and we must do a better job of showing that power at the ballot box.

As a society, we must begin to observe and acknowledge how Black men are excelling under the pressure. And with that understanding, society can provide these men a little more attention, particularly politically, a little more grace, nourishment, strength, and encouragement. Then, we'll see more Black men becoming diamonds.

EPILOGUE

Our baby Sadie was very sick when she was born, and for an excruciatingly long time no one knew if she would make it. Her mother too, after the difficult delivery of our twins, also was fighting for her life. I was praying hard, doing everything I could, but we all know how it is when life is on the line: The dark side of our minds drops hints of disaster, while our stronger spirit, steeled by faith, tries to overcome the darkness with infusions of hope.

Thanks to prayer, my wife's incredible grit, and the amazing, caring Black doctors at Novant Health, outside of Charlotte, who were keen enough to listen to their Black patient, my wife was the first to pull through.

Sadie, however, remained critically ill. Our baby girl was born with a rare liver disease that would place her on the transplant list for months. To be more specific, she was born with a condition called *biliary atresia*, in which a baby's bile ducts are blocked. As her parents, we had no control over whether our newborn daughter would live or die. All we could really do was pray and continue to pray. All Sadie could do was persevere. And she did. She won her battle, eventually receiving a lifesaving liver transplant at the age of eight months.

Sadie is five years old now, and she's a smart, beautiful, and loving little girl. But she was born to fight—she's already gone through more health struggles than many, many older people have ever had to face, certainly more than I have. Today, our daughter is very, very, very particular about everything. She won't move until we place her bows exactly where she wants them. She examines everyone (sometimes even being a little judgmental), for example, offering comments on other people's hair. She'll say, "That's cute." And sometimes we'll even get a sassy, unsolicited "That's not cute." I mean, she's outspoken. She's very free.

To be honest, I don't know if she fully understands what she went through from the time of her birth, or even if she remembers how sick she was. But she behaves like a person who senses that they've already been through hell and back. To this day, she carries on her belly the scar that remains from the transplant operation. And so, every night before settling into bed and after she says her "Now I Lay Me Down to Sleep" prayer, she whispers a pure "thank you" to her liver donor and their family.

I think it's a given that only those who suffer are capable of true appreciation. Black folk in this country, of course, have struggled for centuries, and I pray that most are well aware of the shoulders we stand on, of those who came before us. I'm not nearly as pure as my sweet daughter, but I'm smart enough to know that I wouldn't be where I am today without the sacrifices of Fannie Lou Hamer, Ella Baker, Thurgood Marshall, Rosa Parks, Dr. Martin Luther King, Stokely Carmichael, and Shirley Chisolm, along with my own father and a list of common-folk heroes that's too long to name.

To be honest, though, these days I rarely quote Dr. King. I've moved away from it, mainly because I believe that his legacy has been whitewashed—he's become a holiday, something like St. Patrick, and how many people pause to put down their green beers on March 17 to actually reflect on St. Patrick's good deeds? People regard Dr. King as if he was some docile, peace-loving creature and not the rabid revolutionary he truly was. Do you really know how hard it is to wage peace? Do you understand that a pacifist is in no way passive?

In 1967, Dr. King stepped away from the demands of his grueling schedule to draft what is perhaps his second most important piece of writing: *Where Do We Go from Here: Chaos or Community?* I think about this particular work a lot, even though we all should resolve that his best piece of writing was "Letter from Birmingham Jail." (And if you believe it was the "I Have a Dream" speech . . . well, we're just gonna have to fight about that when I see you later.)

Where Do We Go from Here gave us two choices. He said we could either have chaos or community. I'm sure he drafted this under enormous pressure—it was 1967, after all, and of course he would tragically only have another year to live. His vision in this book is nothing short of prophetic. He calls for better jobs, higher wages, decent housing, and quality education at a time when, even some twelve years after the *Brown v. Board of Education* decision, there were still segregated school districts all over, from Boston to Florida. *Where Do We Go from Here* looks far into the future, on a global scale—it demands an end to global suffering, recognizing that (in the 1960s) humanity *already* had the resources and technology to end poverty worldwide.

When I think on this particular work, I often do so in the context of people born in the year 2000. By the time they took their first steps, these young Americans had already lived through 9/11. They've witnessed a major financial crisis, the Great Recession. They've experienced the election of the first Black president of the United States. They've lived through the advent of the Tea Party, and they've been steeped in the pernicious social poison of MAGA. They came of age during a persistent housing crisis. They've enrolled in colleges and universities, often while swamped in debt. They've lived through Mandalay Bay in Las Vegas, Uvalde, the Pulse night-club, Virginia Tech, Newtown, Parkland, and other shootings that continue to happen—twenty-one of the thirty worst mass shootings in America have occurred since they were born. They've survived church and synagogue shootings, in-cluding the one at the beloved Mother Emanuel AME Church in 2015. Most of them lived through COVID and watched George Floyd struggle to breathe until his last breath. They're now living through Russia's invasion of Ukraine and the dev-astating conflict in Gaza. On top of everything else, the polar ice caps are melting.

Young people today are witnesses to generations of chaos, generations of trauma, and generations of stress just in this one lifetime. And when you think about it from this perspec-tive, we must do two things: give ourselves a little grace and give the leaders of today and tomorrow a little grace as well. We have to embrace our young people in the context of the whirlwind that we have sowed and they have reaped.

Every generation, to be sure, has its traumas. In my own life span, I'd say the cruelest trickery white folk ever played on Black folk was replacing Thurgood Marshall with Clarence Thomas on the Supreme Court. I don't think I'll ever forgive those individuals, some whites and some Blacks, who supported Clarence Thomas. Or the ones who engineered the replacement of the nominated Harriet Miers by Justice Samuel Alito, who made it his life's work to repeal *Roe v. Wade*. I think about people literally saying that Hillary Clinton and Donald Trump were the opposite sides of the same coin, as if one was anything close to the lesser of two evils. And then what happened? Donald Trump appointed three Supreme Court justices! I think about how Mitch McConnell blocked President Barack Obama from his right to appoint a Supreme Court justice, Merrick Garland. I wouldn't doubt that McConnell today considers this the peak of his long and spiteful political career.

* * *

Now, here's what's really scary: I realize that we've probably not yet hit the darkest, rock-bottom moment. Still, Dr. King also taught us that "only when it's dark enough can you see the stars." And so, whenever I contemplate where we'll go from here, I try to see it through the lens of my children, Kai, Sadie, and Stokely. And I remember that this fight is one of righteousness, and one that is just, but it's also one that stretches far back in memory and one that not only continues but has never been broken. When I think about my daughter, Sadie, I think about the late Josephine Wright, who fought until her nineties. I know, as plain as day, that there is no Condoleezza Rice, there is no Nikki Haley, there is no Hillary Clinton, there is no Laphonza Butler, and no Kamala Harris without Shirley

Chisholm—let alone Rosa Parks, who wasn't tired, for good-ness' sake, but *all too tired of giving in.*

So, praise be to Black women, the most bedraggled of us all. My own father admired Ella Baker more than anybody else. I think about the organizing that we must do to stave off the destruction of our country and preserve the fabric of freedom and equity that we aspire to mend by utilizing the strategic stitches left to us by Fannie Lou Hamer, who, inci-dentally, was given a hysterectomy by a white doctor without her consent—what she later derisively called a "Mississippi appendectomy."

Let's talk about Kamala Harris, the vice president of the United States, an empowering figure to young Black girls like Sadie. Despite her stature, however, has any vice president faced the critical onslaught she deals with daily? I find Black women in general are belittled and disrespected, sadly even within Black culture, but these are the heroines I teach Sa-die about. That's my response to Ron DeSantis, and others of his ilk, who would take those lessons away from our brilliant, beautiful Black and Brown children.

* * *

I think there is an unfortunate reality that many parents my age (who are millennials) must recognize, which is that we *still* have not solved the world's problems. Our children are *still* having to grow up in a world that may not be better than the one we inherited. With Sadie, in particular, there is a powerful calm; she's the most resilient person I know, and her mom is the second. They have had to endure all the systemic issues Black people face. It's not just "Oh, your wife almost died in childbirth," but it's "No, she endured a systemic issue that Black women face." It's not just "Oh, your daughter had biliary atresia," but "No, she faced the issues of a flawed transplant system, and we know what people without means and people of color have to go through to deal with those systems."

So, that's the challenge of parents my age: we must understand that we may not get there, but on the flip side, we must know that our children are gifts that *can* get the world there. For example, Sadie's perseverance and strength are gifts she was born with, and these are the precise characteristics her generation will need to confront the darkness we're living through. It will require a certain level of vigor and grit. I think the trouble with all this is that Black folk must have that level of perseverance just in order to survive. My goal for Sadie and Stokely is that they thrive. In fact, my wish for Black folk in general is that one day we can abandon our survival tactics and really learn how to let go and thrive. I believe this new generation can realize this wish for Black America, but it will be tough, because there are determined forces that are hindering progress.

*   *   *

A lot of white folk, including White Men of a Certain Age, fear change. They fear replacement and loss of power, real and imagined. This is obvious, of course, by even a cursory analysis. So, if my generation is going to see change, it's not necessarily going to be due to the rise of Bakari Sellers or Ben Crump, or Alicia Garza or Tarana Burke, or Ibram X. Kendi or Michael Harriot, or Lateefah Simon or Kristen Clarke, or Tiffany Cross or Jason Johnson: No, this change is not on us. It's our burden, but it's not on us, nor is it on Sadie and Stokely's generation.

While we can change our plight as a race of people, this country can't begin to end racism until our elected representatives, prompted by misguided constituencies, stop repealing our rights and liberties. To be blunt, we won't see peace until white evangelical men and women get their shit together and help us to create an equal playing field.

Many of the white folk I meet are concerned about their inheritance and worried about what's being passed down to them or their children. While this is not an indictment of them, let's be real: some of these white folk were born on third base but think they hit a triple. In fact, their preordained destiny was not an achievement—it was their fate. Meanwhile, many of my Black friends and colleagues never even made it to the game. We don't have trusts or estates, the access to wealth, or land, or capital, but this can't be our destiny simply due to the false virtue of skin tone. For Sadie and Stokely, the blessing now is that they don't yet fully understand where they are. They're still believers in Disney, so it's my job not only to continue to fight until there's no breath in me, but to prepare them to take over this world and make it better.

*   *   *

As we look at what history means, or what history tells us, and we examine this moment—with this manufactured anti-Black attack on diversity, equity, and inclusion (DEI) and "wokeness," which I don't even know what that means anymore—when we look at the Supreme Court, and we see that they've taken away a woman's right to choose, that they've ended affirmative action, that they're coming to block Fearless Fund from raising venture capital grants for Black women, the heads of the fastest growing small businesses that have the least access to capital, the rhetorical question becomes: *What's next?*

Well, I believe that what's next is gay marriage. What's next after that is interracial marriage. I believe that there is an attack coming to undo the holding of the 1954 unanimous *Brown* decision. To a certain extent, most of those battles are already underway, which is why I always admonish people for thinking that *this* is the darkest time.

It's not.

It's coming.

But surely darkness must come before the light, which brings me back to our American children, and because of them there's hope. Because of them, the future remains bright. We're trying our very best as parents to do only one thing, which is to raise good human beings. And at the end of the day, we can rail against injustice, we can pass progressive legislation, but the greatest value any of us can create—actually, all that we really know how to do—is to raise our children to live with moral clarity, courage, and strength. I see those stars of Dr. King in Kai, Sadie, and Stokely. I see those stars in their classmates; I see the stars in my nieces and nephews; I see them in all of these young people who are maturing in a more diverse social ecosystem. They've all grown up with somebody who's gay; they've all grown up with somebody who's Muslim; they all know somebody who's Jewish; they all likely know more than one first-generation immigrant.

It's as clear as crystal: the fear of change is not necessarily in them, the fear of the "other" is not coded in their DNA as a response to the intrinsic "Browning of America." Leaning on the lessons of those who came before us—if we manage to pass them down—our children will be able to order their steps. They will create a new America, the one that's already boiling under the surface. America, still the greatest democratic enterprise in the world despite its innumerable flaws, has nevertheless written a check that will not be cashed due to insufficient funds—it may be in ten years, or it may be in twenty, but this new America is rising. Each of us has the ability to continue to push toward its "more perfect union."

The blood of my family, like that of so many others, runs through the soil of this great country, and so I, for one, will continue that battle until there's no more breath in me. And when that time comes, I'm confident that Sadie and Stokely will pick up that baton.

While I think there's something innate about the gifts of courage and leadership that Sadie and Stokely have shown me, even more so I think the hardness of the world they will encounter when they leave our doors, the tribulations and trials they will confront, the toiling in the proverbial vineyard that must be sowed in order to gain success, can harden them or strengthen them or both.

Regardless, it's our job to prepare the young for everything that's headed their way. This new generation has seen the world on fire, so their unique experiences will serve as a springboard to lead all of us to a future of freedom, equality, and maybe even peace.

ACKNOWLEDGMENTS

There are so many people in life who chip in, help you out, and pour into you. But for me, life has been about finding partners. Life has been about a journey and recognizing every day is just a singular step. So here, I start by acknowledging four people who are important in everything I do, who ensure humility but pick me up when I am down:

First and foremost, my wife, Ellen—my partner. She is always there, no matter what. When I look to my left, she is always there; she has my front and back. No one can ask for a better lover, friend, and confidant.

I also want to acknowledge Jarrod, who has been my best friend for some time. Through a year as turbulent and trying as this, Jarrod has been there.

Then, there's Ike. I've known him since what feels like before we were born. His dad was the youngest NAACP state president in the country, and he and my dad were friends before Ike and I were thought of.

Fourth, I want to acknowledge Brian Newman, who was my best friend in the entire world. I say *was* because on January 3, 2023, he died tragically from a clot. It took a lot out of me. The pain never seems to heal. Whether we were at Morehouse, Magic City, or the Pink Pony, we stayed true to each other. We were the epitome of what real friendship looks like.

Brian, I live this life in your memory.

This process couldn't be complete without my editor, Patrik Henry Bass, and publisher and president Judith Curr. In fact, it wouldn't be complete without the entire team over at Amistad and HarperCollins believing in me. It couldn't have been done without Tatsha Robertson helping me day in and day out to hone these thoughts. Thank you, also, Jeff, for helping me get the words down on paper. I appreciate y'all pouring into me, because I am stubborn and still learning and growing. But hopefully the words in this book will mean something to someone somewhere. Much love and light to you all.